1,001 Prayers to Energize Your

Prayer Life

— A JOURNAL —

BARBOUR BOOKS
An Imprint of Barbour Publishing, Inc.

Our mission is to inspire the world with the life-changing message of the Bible.

Member of the
Evangelical Christian
Publishers Association

Printed in China.

Introduction

Does your prayer life feel a little stale? Do you find yourself saying the same things, asking for the same needs, praying over the same situations? Or do you ever sit down, hoping to get closer to God, and find yourself getting closer to dreamland instead? Is your spirit willing, but your flesh weak? Or maybe you've trained your body (head bowed, hands together), but you can't quite get your spirit to settle into talking with God.

Use these words in *1,001 Prayers to Energize Your Prayer Life Journal* as a tool, a catalyst to begin a movement in your heart and spirit. Read the words aloud, silently, or write them down as a prompt to start your conversation with God. There are prayers here designed to address all sorts of human emotions and interactions. If one doesn't fit your particular need in the moment, move on to the next one. You may even want to flag your favorites that you can return to again and again.

Remember, you can pray anywhere and at any time—whether you are standing on a factory floor or climbing on a mountainside, in the heart of a busy city street or in the belly of a whale. God will hear you. He wants to hear you. Why not talk to Him right now?

Devote yourselves to prayer, being watchful and thankful.
COLOSSIANS 4:2

1

Oh Lord, on my own, I am bound to fail. I have done it so many times it feels as though I'm an expert at spiritual nosedives! But when I put my total trust in You, I know I will be victorious. I'm praying for that kind of victory right now.

2

Father God, the joy has gone out of my life. I need Your reassurance that You will never give me a burden without helping me bear it. Be my strong hope for a better future. I will trust You to lead me one day at a time—one moment at a time.

3

Creator God, I love Your sublime handiwork. Your rivers that flow into a glistening sea. The perfect weave of a robin's nest. A sunset lit in gold. Your creation lifts me up. It comforts me. It reminds me that You are in control of the world, my life—and this very moment.

4

Father, how thankful I am that You allow me a "do-over" from time to time! Help me to remember that my friends and family also need those *many* second chances.

5

Thank You, heavenly Father, for giving me all that I need, instead of all that I want. Today I thank You especially for _____.

6

Sometimes at work, at home, and even at church I am confronted with people who are very difficult to love. And sometimes that person who is hard to love—is me. Lord, help me have a humble heart and love others as You would love them.

7

Holy Spirit, You know my spiritual stumbling blocks. You have forgiven me in the past, and I ask You to give me mercy yet again and to show me how to avoid these temptations in the future. I love You, Lord.

8

Thank You, Lord, for all You have given me, for all You have taught me, and for all the good things You've planned for my life. I do not have to worry about the future because I am Your child.

9

I pray that You will transform my mind and show me Your will. When Your purpose is revealed, help me to follow through and do it. I can so easily lose my God-focus with all the distractions of this world.

10

Humans declare, "Might makes right," but I know Your power, Lord, can overcome whatever evil men plan. When I am in despair, fill me with faith in Your justice. Remind me that when trials come, I am more than a conqueror through You, my Savior.

....

....

....

....

....

....

....

11

I often feel that I lack faith, Lord, that You must be speaking
promises for someone else—someone more faithful and deserving
of them. Show me the error of this thinking.

12

Oh God, You are a mighty tower, my fortress, a refuge I can always run to.
In times of trouble, I am comforted to know that You are always on my side.

13

Thank You, Lord, for the abundant life You have given me. I may not always
have a lot financially, but I am so blessed and happy in You. What are some
of the ways I can be wise with my money today so that I please You?

14

Lord, I am human and often tempted. I want to honor You with my life and yet I find
myself straying and not following You as closely as I should. Be with me when I am
tempted, and show me the joy of self-control. I'm listening to Your still, small voice.

15

Lord, I thank You for Your guidance and protection day after day.
Although I never know what the day will bring, You have a
plan for my life, and I choose to trust in You.

16

Lord, I confess that some days my spirit is riddled with doubts concerning You. But my heart cries out to be with You, to know You better, and to trust You fully. Help me in these times of uncertainty. This very day, please strengthen my faith.

17

Thank You, Jesus, for promising me that I don't have to face my troubles alone. You have assured me in Your Word that nothing can separate me from You and Your love. As I go through my days, please give me a supernatural assurance of these truths.

18

Father, I don't know how You will use my life, but I have faith in Your promises and am always ready to do Your will. Amen.

19

Lord, I want You to use me as You see fit. I know that any work You give me to do is an honor. What can we do together today that would give me purpose and bring You glory?

20

Lord, I want my house to be a refuge to those in need. I acknowledge that sometimes having company can be tiring and stressful. Please help me to be a good steward, even on days when I'd rather not share my home or my life with others.

....

....

....

....

....

....

....

....

....

21

Help me invest my time in worthy pursuits, Lord, ones that
will provide lasting satisfaction. I'm not sure what You will ask
me to do, but I am willing to try anything You recommend.

22

Father, I need the courage of a soldier. I feel as though I'm on the front lines of a
battle. Satan would love to see me fail. Please go before me in this spiritual struggle.
Give me supernatural courage that can only come from You. Please help me.

23

Lord, the world is spinning out of control with sin. It would be easier to hide
than to confront evil. When I must fight for what is right, I pray You will
give me the courage to do so. Please give me the right words and actions.

24

Lord, help me be the peacemaker, never the one who stirs up more anger.
You offer peace to me that the world cannot give. Help others to see that peace
in me and long for it themselves. What can I do today to be a peacemaker?

25

Jesus, my Wonderful Counselor, I ask for Your wisdom and guidance.
Instruct me in the ways that I should go. I trust that You will
guide me so I may serve You all the days of my life.

26

Lord, I've learned this—a heart that doesn't feel, cannot be broken. But it also can't love. And a heart that loves can be wounded deeply. You are the great healer, God, and You know how to heal deeply. I ask You now to help me with _____.

27

I know that death comes to us all, Lord, but sometimes I feel I cannot give up a loved one. I know that heaven is a better place, but my grief overwhelms me. Send me Your comfort. Help me remember that grief is the price I must pay for love.

28

At times, I feel as though I'm being tossed to and fro in a sea of anxiety. Even my prayers seem to go unanswered. Oh Lord, please replace my anxiousness with joy. My fear with love. My darkness with hope. I need You more than ever.

29

Lord, give me the strength to forgive others, because sometimes the offense seems too great. Remind me of the lavish grace You have poured out on me so that I may be gracious to others.

30

Oh God, Creator of all things, please allow me to inspire others as You inspire me. What can we create today that might inspire the world?

....

....

....

....

....

....

....

....

....

31

I've seen the most fragile plants survive the hardest frosts. Some days
I feel close to shriveling and dying in this stone-cold world. Oh Lord,
be a blanket of protection over me, and let me not only survive but
once again grow and flourish in Your light and warmth. Amen.

32

The Enemy would like me to look at the Bible as an ancient and outdated book—
one for the shelf. Let me see Your Word for what it is—a living book full of
guidance and grace—one that I can open daily to help me find my way.

33

Conventional wisdom tells me to get out there every day and live large. Lord, I know
You're not impressed with that mind-set. Help me to remember that doing what You
created me to do won't hold me back but bring me to a place of unspeakable joy.

34

I praise You, Father, from the mountaintops—when things go well. It is easy there!
But in those times when things go wrong, help me to praise You still. Give me the
faith to praise You from the valleys of my life, especially _____.

35

Heavenly Father, show me the way to true forgiveness. Help me to forgive
as I have been forgiven. It is not always easy, but it is always Your will for
me in Christ Jesus. Whom do I need to forgive right now?

36

Lord Jesus, draw my family close to You. Fill our home with Your presence
and our lives with Your love. In turn, help each one of us to realize the
importance of blessing others. How can I be a blessing to my family today?

37

Dear heavenly Father, please give me the wisdom I need to properly advise my loved
ones. Help me encourage them to seek guidance from Your Word and in communion
with the Holy Spirit. Help me to be an example as I live out my life before them.

38

Thank You, Lord, for being so faithful. Thank You for Your compassion—
which is just the right amount to get me through the day.

39

Lord, help me to rejoice in the time I have with my family today. I don't want
to dwell on what might happen in the future; I want to relish this chance to
cherish the blessings You've given me. Show me how I can live in the moment.

40

Father, help me realize that my wants are temporary and of little
importance. Let me lean against You, Lord, relaxed in the knowledge
that You will care for me. You know my needs far better than I do.

41

Dear Jesus, You are my dearest friend and my Redeemer. Please don't let me
stray from Your light. And if I have drifted away from any of
Your truths, I ask that the Holy Spirit reveal it to me now.

42

Lord, when You were on earth, You noticed those who went unnoticed by others. You
were a friend of sinners. You gave second chances. You were gracious. You met needs.
You gave until it hurt. Show me how to be a little bit more like You each day.

43

Lord God, in all that I do and say, may my deeds reflect the great love
and grace that You have shown me. In Jesus' name I pray, amen.

44

Lord, I want to love the way You do. I want to speak life into all who cross my path.
I want to show love to those who are less fortunate than I am by giving generously.
I want to care even when it is difficult. How can I have a loving heart today?

45

God, I rejoice in You. I find a hiding place in You. When the world threatens me,
I claim that I am secure as a child of the King. I know that Your protection
is always surrounding me. I will rejoice in You all the days of my life.

46

Forever, Lord—what encouragement there is in that word. We have all eternity to spend with You in heaven. Thank You for this indescribable gift. Thank You for being the Alpha and the Omega, the first and the last. Amen.

47

Lord, You know temptations surround me every day. Help me to avoid situations, places, and people that entice me to stray from Your will. Amen.

48

Lord, I'm grateful that I can turn to You in times of trouble, that I don't have to do this thing called life all by myself. Thank You for Your help and especially for _____. I love You, Lord.

49

When I was young, I recited the prayer, *"God is great. God is good. Let us thank Him for our food."* I remember outgrowing that prayer, and yet, there was a great truth in that little prayer. You *are* great. May I never grow too old to recognize Your greatness.

50

Lord, if there's one thing I need, it is trustworthy guidance. In darkness or light, on fair days or foul, I trust that the light of Your Word will bring me safely home. Praise Your name!

51

Lord, help me to live according to Your guidelines and show my children that Your plan is best as they strive to live for You. I want them to learn to trust You. I cannot teach them these things on my own. I need Your help to raise godly children.

52

Lord, show me my errors and teach me the proper way to take advice. Help me always to seek godly counsel. I can be so stubborn, but I know that I need to receive advice at times in order to make good decisions. Grant me a more open mind and heart.

53

Holy Spirit, give me Your peace and an understanding that all things work together for good when I follow Your will. Amen.

54

Father God, I need Your blessing over my life. As I rise and go about my day, please bless the work of my hands. Make me a blessing to all those who cross my path whether at home or in the workplace. I want to be a blessing to others.

55

Lord Jesus, help me to follow Your example. You said that faith, hope, and love were all important, but You pointed out love as the greatest of all. Help me to love with my whole heart.

56

Dearest Lord, Your Word contains the best parenting instruction and advice I could ever possess. Give me the wisdom to weigh everything else I read against what the Bible says. Thank You for leading me in right paths. Amen.

57

Lord Jesus, I know I'm called to live a godly life, but today I don't feel very righteous. I need Your perfect and holy guidance. I especially need help with _____.

58

God, I do not know how many days I have left on this earth, but I commit them to You. You're my joy and salvation. Even if I cannot do as much as I once could, I will praise You still. You will be my joy even in old age!

59

Lord, when times are hard and I become discouraged, be with me. Keep me a faithful teacher of the Way for the sake of all those to come. May the next generation see You in me.

60

Lord, I know I am Your representative here on earth and should give no one the opportunity to reject You because of my actions. When I am within seconds of being a bad example, send me Your peace and a change of heart.

61

Just as You rescued Your servant David, You reach down and rescue me.
I will praise You for Your wonderful creation, for Your steadfast love,
and for being the one true God. Let me never tire of giving You the
praise that You are due. I praise You now for _____.

62

Lord Jesus, when I am a poor example of Your love to someone I meet,
grant me forgiveness. Grant those I offend the wisdom to understand
that no one is free of sin but that Your grace is sufficient. Amen.

63

Be with all people living alone, Lord. Be especially near to their hearts, I pray.
I think particularly of my friend, _____, who needs Your
tender companionship, Your mercy, and Your love.

64

Holy Spirit, I need an attitude adjustment that can only come from You. Let me be a
cheerful worker instead of a Christian who gets caught sporting an unpleasant 'tude.
I especially need Your transforming power in the area of _____.

65

Lord, help me study Your Word and grow in knowledge of You in order to attain
godliness. Then I can help others around me to understand how to live godly lives.
Help me to place a high priority on reading and applying Your holy Word. Amen.

66

I pray that You will go before me, God. I cannot see more than one step
at a time, but You see the path that You have set me on. You know the
way I should take. Please walk beside me and stay very near to me.

67

As I read Your Word, it is a constant reminder of Your love for me. Please, Lord, let
me see others as You do so that I may love all people as You so dearly love me. Amen.

68

Heavenly Father, let me know when I'm wrong so that I come to You for
cleansing and an opportunity to make things right. Thank You for
the truth in Your Word, even though sometimes the truth hurts.
Please show me if there is an area in which I need to grow.

69

Oh Lord, I find it hard to find time to relax. I admit to being a
workaholic and sometimes a worryaholic! Thank You for making me
to lie down even when I don't want to. Thank You for leading me
beside quiet waters when I need the solace and the peace.

70

Lord, remove the fears that bind me so that I can be happy in the knowledge
that You are there to comfort me—no matter what else is happening.

71

I have no reason to fear, God. I may walk through some tough times. Eventually, I will face the valley of the shadow of death. But I will not face it alone. You are always with me, protecting me, guiding me. I'm so thankful that You are my Good Shepherd.

72

Lord, I want to be instrumental in helping my family establish a close walk with You. Direct me daily to renew my commitment to follow in Your steps. Thank You for being the example I need. Amen.

73

Father, I need rest—rest from my schedule, rest from the demands of my family, rest from "doing" to a place of simply "being." Lead me to that place. Calm my mind and my emotions so I can slow down enough to find real rest. Amen.

74

Lord, You told me to give and that if I do, it shall be given to me. Your generosity is unmatched, and Your blessings are always wonderful. Today, I specifically thank You for the blessing of _____.

75

Lord, I need Your gentle wisdom for every area of life. I'm so thankful that what You offer is the best. What wise understanding can You give me today? I am listening, Lord.

76

Thank You, Father, for the calm assurance that one day I will be with You in heaven. Jesus is preparing a place for me there even now. I am doubly blessed because I have been given this abundant life on earth and eternal life with You in glory. Amen.

77

Father, You gave me my children to cherish, and that includes being gentle with them. I do treasure them, Lord, so help me to impart Your gentleness to them. Amen.

78

Thank You, God, for Your Word. It instructs me on how to live. It brings joy to my days and gives me strength when I am weak. You are my joy. You are my strength. Praise Your holy name!

79

Lord, I'm ashamed to admit that sometimes I have a hard time taking You at Your Word. Please show me how to trust You more, even when my mind can't grasp it and my heart can't accept it.

80

Father, I get discouraged when I don't know which way to go. Remind me that You are right behind me, telling me which way to turn. Help me to shut out the world's clamor and those endless to-do lists so I can listen for Your still, small voice.

81

Lord, I know that even if I walk through the valley of the shadow of death, I will not be shaken. You go with me. You are my hope, and I find my rest and calm assurance in You.

....

....

....

....

....

....

....

82

Father, Your guidance is trustworthy. You are the Good Shepherd.
Thank You for leading me to a place of rest.

83

There's no mistaking it, Lord. You've made it clear that I'm to be joyful
in each and every task. The next time I'm tempted to complain about
the mounds of work—I have the potential to be a royal grouch—
please remind me to turn my murmuring into praise.

84

Gracious Father, I thank You for the work I have. You made work,
and it is part of every person's life. May I do my work in a way
that is pleasing to You and that reflects Your glory. Amen.

85

Father, praising You and rejoicing in You should always be high on
my priority list. Proclaiming Your love to others must never be
lacking in my life. Thank You that I am able to rejoice in You.

86

Lord, I wish that I could say my heart is undivided. I am pulled in so
many different directions lately. I want to meet the needs of so many.
Slow my pace, Father. Speak peace over me now.

....

....

....

....

....

....

....

....

87

Father, I don't know the direction You have for my life, but I have
faith in Your promises and am always ready to do Your will.
I'm so glad we're on this journey together.

88

Lord Jesus, every day of my life You give me opportunities to be about
the work of Your kingdom. Help me to notice that person You would
have me encourage or share the gospel with. Help me to use my
resources and abilities to honor You each day. Amen.

89

Lord, sometimes I need another person to talk to who understands
what I'm going through. Help me find a friend—someone
who needs the kind of companionship I do.

90

Forgive me, Lord, for those times when I've doubted Your love. I know that even
when doors close in my life, You are preparing a way for me—the right way.
Let me rest in You and know that You have good plans for my future. Amen.

91

I am Your ambassador, Lord, and every day I try to show Your love
to those who don't know You. I pray that I will have the
right words and actions today. Guide and direct me.

92

Lord, I want to honor You by bringing up disciplined children. But I need strength in that area. Show me how to be a good and loving parent. And particularly help me when it comes to _____.

93

God, You tell us in scripture that we should clothe ourselves with patience. Still my complaining and anxious heart, oh Lord. Instead of wringing my hands, help me to raise them in praise!

94

Father, my daily problems come and go; yet if I remain steadfast and dedicated, doing the work You have given me to do, I am confident that my reward awaits me in heaven. Give me the endurance that I need to press on in the faith. Amen.

95

Lord, on days when I'm having spiritual struggles, my thoughts become full of discouragement and frustration. I can even suffer from bouts of depression. I don't like to be so controlled by my emotions. Please give me the strength to deal with life. Every day. Every hour.

96

Lord, I can see Your inner power at work in the lives around me. Your Holy Spirit is life changing, and will always be available to us wherever we are. Thank You for this wonderful gift! Amen.

97

I've made mistakes, Lord, too many to count. But someday You will present me faultless, cleansed by Your blood. The evidence of Your power to lift me up and make me whole fills me with exceeding joy.

98

I sometimes want to rely on my own power instead of Yours, Lord. I pray that I will allow You to sit in the driver's seat of my life rather than just ride along as a passenger. Please take control of all areas of my life right now. Amen.

99

Put a new song on my lips, Lord. Let others see me being patient and waiting on You, no matter what difficulty I'm facing. Help them learn the same song of joy that You are giving me.

100

Thank You, Lord, that Your Word is true. Help me to look to Your steady and solid Word, not this world, as my life instruction manual. I thank You that You will never lead me astray, that You never lie to me, and that You always keep Your promises.

101

Lord, may Your character be made visible through my actions. I am so imperfect, and in my humanity, I will continue to make mistakes. Being a Christian is anything but easy. I need Your help!

102

Father, give me faithfulness in all things large and small so that I may be an example to my family, my friends, my coworkers, and all those near me. Amen.

....

....

....

....

....

....

103

Lord, help me realize that my understanding is not necessary for the completion of Your plan. You understand everything; all I need to do is have faith. You will complete the good work You have begun in my life. Please use me in any way You so desire. Amen.

104

Lord God, help me not to judge people but to let You decide the fairness of matters. Give me patience and forgiveness in dealing with others and in dealing with myself. Please help me specifically in the area of _____.

105

Hear the cries of Your people, Father. Just as You did in ancient times. For we are a troubled people and a fallen nation. I pray that we will seek You with a repentant heart. Please deliver us from our sins. In the name of Jesus I pray, amen.

106

Lord, when I see how You have interceded on my behalf, I want to fall on my face before You. My prayers have been answered in miraculous ways. In times when all I could see was darkness, You provided light and power and hope. I thank You, especially for _____.

107

Lord, You are made strong in my weaknesses. Help me to remember that when I'm faced with trials and suffering. I await a wonderful eternity in heaven with You, where all this earthly "stuff" will fade away. I know the things of God are all that really matter.

....

....

....

....

....

....

108

Lord, the next time I am faced with danger for Your sake, let me remember that You are faithful to care for Your people, no matter how much I may fear. Amen.

109

There are times, Lord, when I feel as if You've forgotten me, and I've let those feelings of being forsaken overwhelm me. Help me to remember that You are the Creator of the entire universe, and You hold me in Your strong and merciful hands!

110

Lord Jesus, I know we give praise to many people and things that are unworthy. Remind me when I begin to stray that You are the one true God and the only one who is truly worthy of our praise. Amen.

111

Thank You for Your promise to preserve me if I love You, Jesus. I know that this is an eternal promise. What more incentive do I need to pursue a right walk with You? Keep me on the right path, Lord. Lead me today in all that I do, all that I say.

112

Thank You, Jesus, for Your sacrificial love for me. Thank You for the example of true love that You have provided. May I be crucified with You and allow You to reign in my heart and live through me. Amen.

113

Lord, You know how painful it is when things are not right between friends. What a joy it is to know that I am made right with You by faith. We can communicate freely, talking and listening, enjoying each other as heart friends. Thank You for restoration and righteousness.

....

....

....

....

....

....

114

Lord, when I feel alone and helpless, remind me that You know me fully and love me deeply. You even know the number of hairs on my head. Thank You that You will walk with me all the days of my life. You will never leave me or forsake me.

115

Father, please don't let me fall into the trap of false pride. Whatever beauty I bring into this world is only a tiny reflection of Your beauty, Your creation, Your perfection. May my worth always come from within, where You abide in my heart. Amen.

116

Father, as long as I trust in You, I have nothing to worry about. Nothing can separate me from You, because You are the strong protector, the mighty one who watches over me always. I praise You, Lord, for Your protection.

117

Holy Spirit, bring me opportunities to comfort others as You comfort me. Help me to be ready to reassure and encourage a child or a friend, an aging parent or even a complete stranger who is in need. Is there someone You have in mind today? I'm right here, listening.

118

God, I can't begin to count the number of times You've wrapped Your loving arms around me and calmed me in the midst of fears. You've drawn me near in times of sorrow and given me assurance when I've faced great disappointment. I thank You with all my heart.

119

Heavenly Father, I want my family and friends to serve You, but I know they can only do that if they have true faith in You. Help me live so that they will want this kind of faith. Amen.

....

....

....

....

....

120

Dear Jesus, on days when I go off by myself—and I seem
determined to do my own thing—please draw me close
to You until I calm down and begin to think clearly.

121

Lord, You are my hope in an often hopeless world. You are my hope of heaven,
my hope of peace, my hope of change, purpose, and unconditional love. Fill the
reservoir of my heart to overflowing with the joy that real hope brings. Amen.

122

God, my hope is in You from the moment I wake up in the morning until
I lay my head down on my pillow at night. Please give me the ability to
find hope even in situations that may seem hopeless. I especially
need Your hope when it comes to _____.

123

When I grow old, Lord, I pray that I will see the fruits of my labor and rejoice,
knowing that all my efforts were well worth my time and energy. Help me not
to dread old age, and help me not to waste the time You've given me. Amen.

124

When grief over the deaths of those I love comes to me, Father, I know
You understand my suffering and long to comfort me. I am thankful that
I do not grieve as those who have no hope. My loved ones who accepted
You are in a glorious place now! Thank You for that promise!

125

Lord, You've given us plenty of instruction on parenting, and it's because You know what's best. Thank You for seeing the need to include parenting in Your Word. Help us to follow Your ways as we parent our children. Amen.

126

Jesus, Your promise of protection gives me a secure feeling. I'm surrounded by Your loving and sheltering arms. Remind me of these truths when the Enemy tries to harm me and fill me with fear and doubts.

127

Lord, thank You for Your gift of physical pleasures, but teach us to use them wisely, according to Your wishes for us. Keep us faithful to our spouses and to Your laws of self-control. Help us not to entertain even the idea of adultery. Amen.

128

Lord, show me the path to victory every day, because sometimes I find it hard to follow. Make my paths straight as I acknowledge You as Lord of my life. I ask these things humbly in the name of Your Son, Jesus. Amen.

129

Thank You for the work You have given me, Father, with its opportunities to be of service to others and to You. What work do You have for me today, Lord? I'm listening.

130

God, so many times I rush into my day headlong without stopping to spend time in prayer. Remind me that I should lift up my day and my very soul to You before I take one step.

131

Lord Jesus, You have paid for my salvation through Your death on the cross; You made me a child of light that I might guide others to You. You have made me worthy, and I thank You. Help me to shine for You in the darkness of this world. Amen.

132

Lord, I want to obey You in everything and also lead others to obey You. Through my obedience to You, help me to reach many people for Your kingdom. Amen.

133

God, You are the giver of all good things. You withhold no precious gift from Your children. Just as an earthly father longs to give to his children and provide for them, You long to bless us. I specifically thank You for the gift of _____.

134

I'm not always joyous, Lord. To be honest, sometimes I'm downright depressed. Please replace my sorrow with songs of joy. I may have to sing for a while before the joy takes root. I want to learn to be content and joyful in all circumstances, especially in the area of _____.

135

Today in anger, I said something I shouldn't have. Forgive me, Lord. Instead of speaking in anger and frustration, I want to fill my mouth with words of continual praise to You. Even when I feel angry, I do not have to sin. Set a watch over my lips, Father.

136

Lord, thank You for Your attention to those who struggle. I don't always understand Your ways. They're higher than mine. When I question Your provision, I question Your sovereignty. Help me to trust that You remain Jehovah-Jireh, the one who provides, regardless of the timing or methods You choose.

137

Lord, one of the greatest gifts You've given me is the Holy Spirit to intercede for me during prayer. Thank You, Holy Spirit, for intervening and making my requests better than I ever could. Amen.

138

I want to follow You not with just part of me but with all my heart. Hold me close, Father. Do what it takes in my life to get me to the point of full surrender. I want to mean it when I say that I surrender all. Amen.

139

Lord, help me to redefine greatness for the young people in my life and to show them worthy examples of those who have received You. They need to know that there is a better, more glorious way to live.

140

Lord, I know that Your blessings are forever and I have nothing to fear. Please give me a merry heart so that others will be drawn to me. After all, nobody likes a grumbler. And remind me that if there's a smile in my heart, it should show on my face!

141

Lord, in the heat of anger, control my tongue, because what I say then can be as damaging to my soul as it is to my victim's reputation. Remove from me the temptation to gossip, for no good comes from this. Make me faithful in all things, Lord. Amen.

142

Jesus, I know You stand before the throne of Your Father and claim me
as Your own, exempt from sin and judgment. Because You were presented
as the spotless Lamb of God, I'm seen as righteous by my Father.
He sees me through a "Jesus lens." Praise Your holy name!

143

God, sometimes I sin without meaning to do so. Other times I follow
Satan's detour willingly. This can bring great destruction to my life.
I have seen it in others' lives as they've crumbled away. I don't want
this for my life. Keep me from willful sin, I pray. Amen.

144

Lord, I long to be more connected to You. Teach me to worship You as the
true source of power and love. I adore You like no other. Transform me
so my prayers will be powerful and my life will be fruitful.

145

Lord, here I am before You. I'm ready to "take up my cross" and follow You. Every day
I want to be with You, empowered by You, and loved so deeply that I am changed.
Show me what it means to lose my life in order to save it. Amen.

146

Thank You, Lord, for putting other godly people in my life. They face many
temptations and struggles that I face, but they've committed themselves
to purity and godliness, so together we can encourage one another.
What a blessing it is to have a circle of Christian friends.

....

....

....

....

....

....

....

147

Lord, so many times I am tempted to think that people or things will satisfy me. But often they leave me empty and unfulfilled. Help me to remember that You are the source of my hope—not a finer car, or a better job, or that second slice of pie!

148

Thank You, Lord. You have given me a wonderful example of patient endurance. When I am losing patience, I recall how long You waited for me to repent and turn to You.

149

Lord, now that I am devoted to You heart and soul, I am a new creation. Thank You for washing away my old ways of thinking and behaving and for empowering me to live a new life. Your love changes me!

150

Father, when someone does me wrong, I want that person to admit it and ask for forgiveness. From Your patience with me, I know there are times when I need to wait for someone's apology. Help me to wait, Lord. Amen.

151

Thank You for the times when I am humbled, Lord. You are always here— to listen, to forgive, and to heal. Lord, help me to be repentant, to be willing to be brought low. Heal me of quick-temperedness and selfishness. Heal this waywardness in me, especially in the area of _____.

152

Lord, when I'm old, I want to be respected and loved. By my actions toward others, I'm always teaching—either respect or disrespect. I want to set the right example for the next generation as I honor older people. Help me to see and use those teachable moments wisely.

153

Humble me, Lord. Fill me with the desire to listen to my parents. I can learn so much from them and benefit from their life experiences. I believe this is Your will. Thank You for Your patience and guidance. Amen.

154

God, living in this society is like living too near a volcano that's ready to blow. I want to build my house on the stability of Your Word. I want to follow Your will, not the wishes of this world. Help me in this endeavor, every day, every hour.

155

Lord, what a blessing You are that You have given us such an array of emotions with which to express ourselves. Help me to be more like You—slow to anger and abounding in love. Help me to be a person who is merciful and forgiving. Amen.

156

Holy Spirit, we live in a world that lifts up proud people. Make us all aware of how much You value sacrifice. Help us to have the humble spirit we need when we come before You—just as I do now.

157

Thank You, Jesus, for calling sinners to repentance. If You had come only for the righteous, I would not have been called, for I am a sinner. I thank You for Your mercy. Amen.

....

....

....

....

....

158

Lord, I want to grow up spiritually. I want to move from head knowledge to heart experience with You. I want to know what it means to enjoy Your presence, not just to make requests. Step-by-step and day by day, teach me to follow and learn Your ways.

159

Lord, the world is confused about what is evil and what is good. This is surely the result of ignoring Your Word, abandoning the church, and not spending time communing with You. Forgive us, Jesus, for we have sinned greatly as a nation. Please bring us back to You. Amen.

160

Lord, there is so much I do not understand about You. Still, I can see the effects of Your actions, the evidence that You are still active in my daily life. I do not need to physically see You to believe. Your evidence is everywhere.

161

Lord Jesus, the life I am living right now is the result of Your immeasurable and extravagant love for me. Thank You for Your great sacrifice on the cross, which has saved me and made me whole. Amen.

162

Lord, Your compassion for people is great. Create in me a heart of compassion; enlarge my vision so I see and help the poor, the sick, the people who don't know You. Whom do You want to place on my heart today?

163

Lord, help me to show compassion toward my children and offer wise instruction. You are the best example of good parenting, so please show me how to raise my kids. Amen.

164

Lord, I can no longer hide in the darkness of my guilt and sin. You already know everything I've done wrong, yet You bring me into the light—not to condemn, nor to condone, but to heal me. I acknowledge my wrongs and confess them all to You now.

165

Jesus, thank You for Your gift of eternal life and the power to do Your will. I cannot fathom how You suffered, yet You did it all for me—for every person. You bled for my sins. You had victory over death. You made a way for me.

166

Lord, Your Word is a lamp in my darkness—a flashlight on the path of life that helps me to see the way. Your words enlighten me with wisdom, insight, and hope, even when I cannot see where I am going or how things will turn out. Thank You, Lord.

167

Almighty God, it is hard for me to fathom that You spoke all this into existence— the trees and flowers of all kinds, animals in all their uniqueness, even human beings. Help us to be wise stewards of Your creation. Amen.

168

Lord, You are my strength and my song. Help me teach others to sing, no matter what is going on around us. I want us to make a joyful noise to You, Jesus, the author and finisher of our faith. Amen.

169

Lord, I pray for Your power to sustain me as I take care of myself—by eating healthy food and exercising. Please keep me from injury and illness. When I do suffer illness, Father, I pray that You will use that time to draw me closer to You.

170

God, self-control is not one of my strengths, and I need to work on it.
Help me turn things over to You and allow You to develop self-control
in my life, especially concerning my inability to _____.

171

Lord, there's so much chaos. Quiet my spirit. Let me close my eyes for a moment
and experience Your touch. My strength comes from You, not from any other
source. Calm me. Keep me anchored in You and Your Spirit. Amen.

172

God, no one else can see my heart. They may get glimpses of it through my words or
actions. They may grow to know me over the years. But You are my Creator. You knit
me together in my mother's womb. You know my heart. Make it pure, oh Lord.

173

Lord, when I first considered starting a family, I thought I would be a perfect parent.
It was easier dreamed than done. I know I need Your assistance if I'm going to be a
good parent. I specifically need guidance in the area of _____.

174

Because of Your strength, Lord, I can smile. When I need peace, You strengthen
me on the inside. This is where I need You the most. I am not strong on
my own, but in You, oh Lord, I am more than a conqueror!

175

Lord, I know bad things will come my way in life, but I'm secure in Your
love, which never fails. I'm constantly blessed by Your care and concern.
Remind me that even though I am not immune to the troubles of
mankind, You have already overcome this world! Amen.

176

Father, physically, I'm wearing out. But in the core of my being, in my heart,
I still feel strengthened by You. What a blessed promise, that this
inner strength will be my portion forever. Amen.

177

God, the word *awesome* has become overused in our society. We call everything
from football teams to musical artists awesome. You, God, the Creator
of all and Redeemer of my heart. . .You are truly awesome!

178

Lord, I thank You that You are my true companion—that I am never alone. You have
assigned angels to watch over and protect me. You have given me Your Holy Spirit
and promised that You are with me always, even to the very end of the age.

179

Lord, I ask that You would establish our home on the solid rock of Your love. Be our
cornerstone. May our family be rooted in love, grounded in grace, and rich in respect
for one another. May we stand firm as a family built on a foundation of true faith.

180

Lord, I know there will come a day when we will be in heaven with You. I look
forward to that time. Just like the criminal who died on the cross next to Yours,
I will be with You in paradise because I believe in You. What a promise!

181

Father, there comes a time when our parents begin to need help. Give me
the wisdom to understand the problems they are having and to recognize
the often-simple ways I can be of service to them. Amen.

182

Lord, be our strong defense and protect our home. May this be a place of safety,
comfort, and peace. Guard us from outside forces and protect us from harmful
attacks from within. I pray that the Holy Spirit would put a hedge
of protection around our home and family. Amen.

183

Lord, thank You for the joy of celebration! Help us to be a family that remembers
and gathers together—not just for birthdays and holidays, but even to celebrate
the little blessings of life. We are thankful for all that You have done in our lives.

184

In the midst of suffering, I want to keep my eyes on You, Jesus. The suffering You
endured for my sake makes my trials look like nothing. Help me to look forward
to the promise of eternal life and to forget the temporary troubles I have now.

185

Lord, it seems odd to consider trials a joyful thing. But I pray that my challenges in
life, these times of testing, will lead me to greater perseverance. May that perseverance
finish its work so I will be mature and complete and on my way to wholeness.

186

Lord, I ask for Your help when it comes to getting along with my family. Teach me to focus on their good points and on the good times we've had together, not the bad, for the sake of family peace. Thank You for adopting us into Your family. Amen.

187

Lord Jesus, I admit that we humans fail one another. It just comes with the territory of living in a fallen world. I thank You for Your unfailing love. It's unconditional and the same yesterday, today, and tomorrow. I rejoice as Your child that I can always count on You.

188

Dear God, thank You for Your words that speak to my heart and needs. Your life-giving messages are like rain showers on new, green grass. Today I am in need of more than a sprinkle. I need a downpour—a soaking, abundant rain in my dry heart!

189

Father, Your correction lasts only a moment, but the blessings are eternal. When I realize You are so concerned for me and want to help me, I'm filled with gratitude and willing to be led in the right direction. You discipline me as parents discipline their children, out of love.

190

God, my responsibility as Your child is to share the gift of salvation with others. So many need to hear the Gospel. Make me attentive to each opportunity You present to me. Is there someone You'd like me to reach out to today? I'm listening for Your voice.

191

Father, I pray I will be able to bear death as well as I bore life, secure in Your love and looking to the salvation that You have promised is mine. Amen.

192

You are the one true God. You are the great I Am, faithful in every situation to be what we need You to be. You provide. You sustain. You forgive. You teach and guide and even discipline Your children in love. I praise Your name today and forevermore!

193

Dear Giver of dreams, I believe You've placed dreams within me that are yet to be realized. Teach me to delight myself in You as I pursue the desires of my heart. Show me Your perfect will. May I move as far and as fast as You wish. Amen.

194

Please cleanse me from my ungrounded fears, Lord. Fill me with a confidence in You that I can share with others. You are the strong protector. We will rest in Your almighty arms.

195

Lord, show me what convictions to establish, and give me the strength to stand firm in those convictions. Even if an activity or custom is permissible, it may not be of benefit. Help me to be discerning as I make my daily decisions. I ask this in Jesus' name, amen.

196

Lord, may those I work with always see You in my life and be brought closer to You through me. I never want to be a stumbling block but always a beacon of light that leads others to You. Please give me opportunities for spiritual conversations as I go through my day.

197

Thank You for Your promise to guide me in all things great and small.
Your eye is always on me, keeping me from error and ensuring
that I can always find a way home to You.

198

Lord, I commit my aspirations to You. Give me the courage to work toward my goals
and not be swayed by the opinions of others. Renew my mind and spirit so I'll be
able to test and approve what Your will is—Your good, pleasing, and perfect will.

199

Lord, I do not know how to deliver myself from temptation, but You
know the way. You have been there. When I stumble, I know Your arms
will catch me; if I fall, You bring me to my feet and guide me onward.
I specifically need deliverance in the area of _____.

200

Lord, I receive the love gift of salvation, knowing that it is by grace
that I have been saved, through faith. I didn't do anything to
deserve it or earn it. Praise You for Your mercy and love!

201

Lord, You have given me a peace that allows me to live confidently in this world. Even
if people disagree with my beliefs, even if I am persecuted or belittled, I will rest in
Your peace. Nothing has the power to come against me, because I am Your child.

202

Lord, forgive me when I treat my family members poorly. Show me their
good points, for I have overlooked or forgotten many of them. For our
sake, help me bring peace, forgiveness, and love to my family. Amen.

....

....

....

....

....

....

203

Lord, You created all things. You are the Creator of the universe.
You are the Sovereign God of the world, worthy of glory and honor.
May Your holy and mighty name be praised forever and ever!

204

Father, when it comes to money matters, I cannot approach perfection, but I know
that with Your help I can learn to handle my finances faithfully. Guide me in
Your wisdom, and set before me wise counselors as needed. Amen.

205

Jesus, I need Your times of refreshment. Bread of heaven, as You nourish
my body with food, feed my soul with Your words of comfort and life.
May I be filled with Your healing love, joy, and goodness. I sit quietly
in Your presence now with wonderful anticipation.

206

Lord, sometimes I feel like my emotions need a makeover. Renovate me—
transform me so I can be balanced and healthy emotionally. I ask for
Your power to change. I don't want to be the way I used to be.
I want to be wise and enjoy sound thinking. Amen.

207

Father, sometimes I have to go against the wishes of others to do Your will.
It's not always pleasant, but Your wishes come before all others. I will do
my best to honor Your name every day of my life. Please show me the way.

208

Lord, I know that You are the one at work in me; Your Spirit is part of me, and You guide my thoughts and actions. Thank You, Lord God, for that supernatural gift!

209

Please, Lord, help me to make wise decisions and to be a good steward of myself, the "temple" You have given me. Help me not to abuse my body but to care for it as You would want me to. I especially need help when it comes to _____.

210

Lord, I admit I sometimes wring my hands with worry. Show me how to cast my cares at the foot of Your throne and not pick them back up every hour. Or every five minutes! I want to trust fully that You can handle all my concerns.

211

Father, my heart is breaking over the death of a beloved Christian friend. Fill me with Your comfort and the joy that comes from knowing that when death does come, You will be there to guide us home to You. I claim the comfort that You promise in Your Word. Amen.

212

Lord, I need more joy in my life. Daily living and trials can be so depleting and even depressing; I just can't do it on my own. Help me to laugh more and enjoy life again. Help me to have a childlike, playful spirit—a lighter heart.

213

Father, quite often I pray for what is impossible. But for You, nothing is impossible. Even where there seems to be no way, You can make a way. Help me to trust in You to do the impossible in my life. In Jesus' name I pray, amen.

214

Lord, thank You for the peace that restores me and brings wholeness.
When my heart is restless, my health suffers. But when I am at peace,
You restore my entire body. I can breathe easier, and I can smile again
because I know everything's going to be all right. Amen.

215

Heavenly Father, I pray that all Your children will love Your Word and understand
how special they are to You and how You have something for each of them to
meditate on every day. Draw us close to You, Father. Help us to glorify You.

216

Lord, thank You for asking Jesus to pay the high price for what I've done.
The thought of His sacrifice and Your unending grace humbles
me beyond words. "Thank You" will never be enough.

217

Father, give me eyes to see the unique gifts and personalities of each member
of my family. Help me to appreciate their dreams even if they are not
my own. Help me not to give in to the temptation of being bossy,
but to offer gentle guidance, love, and support! Amen.

218

Lord, I'm so worn-out. Help me sleep well at night. I ask for more energy during the
day and a more vibrant spirit. Lighten my load so I can have a better balance between
my work, ministry, and home life. Replenish me, Lord, as I rest in Your presence.

219

Lord, thank You for giving me hope. I don't know what the future holds, but You give me the ability to be joyful even while I wait. Please help me to live with a mind-set of patience and courage as You work Your will in my life. Amen.

220

Lord, Jesus, we are a hurt nation—an angry nation struggling to maintain its values while still dealing firmly with those who hate us. Guide our nation's leaders during these difficult times. We trust in You and long for Your divine guidance and peace. Amen.

221

Lord, may I never hesitate to forgive anyone when You have already forgiven me. I am so blessed to be forgiven and made right with You.

222

Father, help me to have patience, knowing my season is coming, according to Your timetable, and trusting that with Your help every fruit I produce will be good. Amen.

223

Through Your holy Word, Lord, my soul is fed and nurtured. With Your living Word—the Bible—I am made vibrant, hope filled, and alive!

224

Lord Jesus, I thank You for all the times when You have rescued me. I pray that I'll always remember Your ways and walk in them. I desperately need Your help to survive and thrive in this dark world. You're my helper and my gracious, loving, sovereign God. Amen.

....

....

....

....

....

....

....

225

Lord, You are called Wonderful Counselor because You freely give wisdom and guidance. You are the mighty God, the one who made the entire world and keeps it all going. My everlasting Father, it's Your love and compassion that sustain me. My Prince of Peace, I worship and honor You!

226

Through You, Lord, I can live a life that will give others no right to accuse me of any wrongdoing. I pray that You'll allow my life to be an example that will encourage my family, my friends, and others to come to You. Amen.

227

Lord, help me to overcome the urge to pat myself on the back in the sight of others. I admit I love the attention it brings. Give me a desire, instead, to do good for the sake of doing good and not for praise from those around me.

228

Lord, I want our family to pray together more often. We need to put You first because You are the source of life—and You are worthy of our firstfruits of time and attention. Help us make spending time with You a priority. Amen.

229

You are the great Redeemer. You bring beauty from ashes. You take what was dead and make it alive. You use broken vessels. You can use even me. I am so thankful for the redemption You provide, oh God.

230

Lord, thank You for the gift of laughter! Thank You for the joy You bring into my life through a child's smile, a luscious peach, a hot shower, a good night's sleep. Help me remember all these delights when I am looking up at You.

231

Vows to You must be kept, Father. You not only remember Your promises to us, You never forget our promises to You. Help me treat my vows to You seriously, Lord. If sacrifices are required of me, let me bear them in faith. Amen.

232

Father, my heart is breaking. I need to know that You are near and that You care. Gently remind me that You have the power to heal every hurt and help me make it through what I'm facing right now.

233

Lord, give me the resolve to make things better, to ignore my pride, and to do whatever is needed to restore the harmony in my family. We are a Christian family, and we need to be an example to others and a light in the world. I pray for harmony and peace now.

234

Lord, rescue me from my sea of doubt and fear. I don't want to be like an ocean wave that is blown and tossed by the wind. Please quiet my stormy emotions and help me believe that You will take care of me. Amen.

235

Lord, thank You for filling the earth with a bounty of food. Help me to eat nutritiously, to drink enough water, and to avoid overindulging. Temptations are always there, especially _____, but I know You can help me to be disciplined.

236

Father, I admit that once in a while I have a temper tantrum, disputing Your guidance and wanting my own way; but You have never been wrong. Thank You for Your love and patience with me, for I will always need Your guidance, especially when it comes to _____.

237

Lord, keep me on the right path when my own plans are flawed, because only You know where You need me to be today and tomorrow. Make my paths straight, and steer me clear of any way that would lead me to destruction, I pray. Amen.

238

Lord, I often make mistakes on the path of life, losing sight of the trail and calling out for You. Thank You for finding me, for putting my feet back on the path and leading me home.

239

God, I often go about my days unaware of the traps that Satan is setting. He would love to see me stumble and fall. He wants to lure Your children away from You. Please protect me from his evil schemes. Be my refuge always. Amen.

240

God, help untangle my emotions and sort my jumbled thoughts. Calm my restless spirit. Ease my anxieties. Help me experience Your supernatural peace in a real and tangible way. I know that true peace can come only from You, heavenly Father.

241

Heavenly Father, I long for Your peace in my heart. Please take every anxious thread, every tightly pulled knot of uncertainty, sorrow, conflict, and disappointment into Your gentle, loving hands. You are always enough for me. I am so thankful to be Your child. Amen.

242

Lord Jesus, when happiness is hard to come by, help me to learn to draw more consistently on Your wellspring of joy. Help me delight in the little gifts and simple pleasures You bring my way every day.

243

Your Word says that salvation is found in no one else but Jesus Christ. Our society likes to try to convince me that I can find life in other ways. I choose to believe not in other gods or in other religious philosophies or in materialism, but in You alone, Lord.

244

God, I wake up with anxiety at times. I fear the future, and I want to slow down the hands of time. Please calm my racing mind and whisper to me a calm assurance that You have everything under control. Thank You, Father. Amen.

245

Oh God, help me think before I speak. Put words of kindness in my mouth that will build up others instead of destroying them. I desire to be virtuous and to please You in all I do and say.

246

Lord, if I trust You for my eternal salvation, why don't I trust You for my daily needs? Like the Israelites who gathered more manna than they needed, I worry about the future instead of trusting You. Instill in me a trust that You will meet each need as it arises.

247

Father, don't let me feel social pressure when giving. No matter how much or how little I can give, help me to give joyously and with a cheerful heart. Amen.

248

God, just as Joseph found favor with You in Pharaoh's courts and was blessed by Your hand, I pray that I will find favor with You as well. May I walk in Your ways and be blessed by Your hand all the days of my life. Amen.

249

Lord, plant Your wisdom in me like seeds in the soil. Help me cultivate each one and follow Your ways. They're pure, peace loving, considerate, submissive, full of mercy and good fruit, impartial, and sincere. May I be a person who sows in peace and raises a harvest of righteousness. Amen.

250

Lord, the next time I am angry, guide me away from sin until I can speak words of peace and comfort once again. Give me the strategies I need in order to refrain from sinning when I am angry. I want to be kind even when I am frustrated. Amen.

251

Lord, when my family is treated unfairly or when someone judges me before knowing the whole story, I want to see justice done. Remind me to rely on You for that justice. Only You have the power to set things right once and for all. Amen.

252

Lord Jesus, every day is a battle. I struggle between following You and choosing what feels right in the moment. I need Your wisdom and power to persevere toward a true change of heart and action. But most of all, I need Your forgiveness, especially in the area of _____.

....

....

....

....

....

253

Heavenly Father, the world is a frightening place. I look around and see endless opportunities for disaster and tragedy. Please protect me and my family from harm and evil. I place my trust in You. Amen.

254

Lord, I know I can't hope to escape every unpleasant circumstance in this world. Just the same, I will trust in You, whatever comes. Protect me in the way You see fit, in the way that best advances Your purpose for my life. Amen.

255

Open my eyes and reveal to me what You want me to glean from Your Word, Lord. I know that You want me to sit at Your feet and learn from Your teachings. Thank You for the Bible, which is my instruction manual for life.

256

Lord, when it comes to courage, I have none of my own. Without You, I would be filled with fear, terrified of a future I cannot see. Thank You for patiently taking my hand and helping me face my fears. Amen.

257

Father, on my worst days I feel totally unworthy. But I know You have promised to cleanse me from all unrighteousness, to wipe away my guilt and make me whole if I confess my sins. Please forgive me for _____.

258

Lord, life seems overwhelming to me sometimes. Please give me the wisdom You've promised and help me to relax in the knowledge that You will guide me. I take great comfort in knowing that if I ask, You will give me wisdom. I am asking, Father.

....

....

....

....

....

....

259

Father, I know it is Your will for me to understand Your Word, and You've given me the Holy Spirit to guide me. Help me to take advantage of this great blessing. Amen.

260

Lord, guard my tongue. Season my speech with grace—to encourage others and lead them to walk in Your path. When they have questions, I pray that You supply the answers. Amen.

261

There's so much hustle and bustle all around me, Father. Help me to find quiet times even if I must rise much earlier or stay up later. Examine my heart and point out to me where I'm wrong. I especially need to grow in the area of _____.

262

Lord, there are many forces in the world that are coming against me. Your Word says that there is nothing in heaven or on earth that can separate us from Your love. Thank You for Your wonderful reassurance.

263

Lord, as I read and study Your Word and hear sermons preached about it, I still have questions and much to learn. I ask that You give me a clear understanding of Your Word.

264

I'm ashamed to admit that I often speak before I think, and the words that come out of my mouth are anything but wise. Help me to be wise enough to think first then speak. Please help me to be a good example for others. Amen.

265

You're a good Father, and I am loved by You.
Grant me good judgment and teach me Your ways.

266

Lord, there are many times when I need You and Your Word to guide me.
Lead me and help me become an overcomer. You tell me in Your Word
that I am more than a conqueror through Jesus Christ, Your Son. Amen.

267

There is no condemnation for us when we believe in You, Jesus. The covering
of Your blood helps us to prevail over anything. We never need to fear
anymore. Thank You for giving us this victory. My sins are washed
away because You died for me. Praise Your name!

268

Lord, help me to forget the things in my past that I need to leave behind. Give me
courage to press on. Help me to face forward and march boldly into the future.

269

Lord, the fabric of our society has been unraveling for some time.
Help our nation to call on Your name, seek Your face, and turn from our
wicked ways—so You will forgive our sins and heal our land. Amen.

270

Lord, I pray for each member of my church—that we would get along.
Despite our variety of backgrounds and opinions, help us to live and worship
in harmony. Protect us against divisions, and help us to be like-minded. Amen.

271
When all hope seems lost, Lord, be with those who suffer. Be with those who are just about to give up today. Renew their minds. Help them to never abandon hope, for all things are possible with You.

272
Lord, help me hold on to hope. Abraham had great faith in You and became the father of many nations. Though he was old, You provided a son for him and his wife, Sarah. As You did for them, please fulfill my longings—and Your vision for my life's purpose.

273
Lord, I've prayed, and healing hasn't come. It's hard to know why You do not heal when You clearly have the power to do so. But I do know that You will heal me either here on earth or in heaven one day when You give me a new body.

274
Sometimes, Father, I sense Your protection and Your blessing. God, I pray that You will continue to surround me with Your favor. I need You every day, every hour, every moment.

275
Lord, show me all the good You have done for the faithful throughout history, and give me some of Your strength when my own fails. Let my dependence on You turn weakness into strength. Amen.

276

Lord, may our city leaders lead with integrity, honesty, and fairness. Help these people to lead with justice, grace, and mercy: the mayor, our judges and court officials, members of the police and fire departments, and other civic leaders. Amen.

277

Lord, Your love is so strong that You swept down to snatch me from the gravest times of my life. You know how hard things have been; I thought I was going to die. But I didn't. And it's all because of Your power of deliverance. I praise You, Lord!

278

Father, my trials are not major, so far. But I know that things can go wrong in an instant. When I cry to You, I know You hear. Thank You for Your promises and Your never-ending care.

279

Help me, God, not to seek revenge. When someone hurts me, I know that You see the pain. Help me to leave the judgment to You, trusting that in Your perfect justice and mercy, You will make all things right one day. Amen.

280

Lord Jesus, I pray You will always be my Rock, my salvation. Hear me when I call to You for help, for I know You love me. Amen.

281

Father, when I hear myself belittle or speak harshly to my spouse, remind me to show love every day. I want to honor You in my marriage even on days when this is not an easy task. I especially need help when it comes to _____.

282

Lord, give me wisdom and strength in my instruction to my children.
Help me to be firm when I need to be, yet full of compassion.

283

Heavenly Father, I have so much to be grateful for. My list of blessings
is never ending. May I never fail to praise You for Your many blessings.
Today I especially want to thank You for _____.

284

Father, teach us the importance of self-control, how not to give in to the temptation
of sin. Only when we turn from sin can we truly gain understanding in
all wisdom. We ask for Your strength to help in this. Amen.

285

Lord, fill me with compassion for my fellow Christians so I might be a godly example
of love and understanding. I want to emulate You, Jesus, in all I do and say.

286

Lord, no matter what happens to upset me on the surface, You are in my
innermost being, bringing peace and comfort. Thank You that I can
always trust You, even in the midst of life's greatest storms. Amen.

287

God, I'm so weary. I've been through so much. Day after day, I agonize. I am
anxious about the future. I call out to You. Father, set my feet on solid ground.
You are the Rock of my salvation. I know that I can stand if You stand with me.

288

Lord, I feel like a withered plant with dry, brown leaves. Help me connect with You in prayer so I can grow strong and healthy like a vibrant green tree. You are my source of living water!

289

There are days when I don't know how much longer I can go on. But Your Word says that You will provide a way of escape. You help us overcome our temptations. Thank You for Your promises. Praise Your holy name!

290

Father, many temptations come from evil forces that are so deceptive they are hard to see. The devil fights against us daily. Thank You for providing a way that we can be protected from the full assault of Satan's deceitfulness. Amen.

291

Lord, I am weary. Infuse me with life, energy, and joy again. I don't have to look to a favorite food or the compliments of a friend to fill me up on the inside. Steady and constant, You are the one who fills me and loves me.

292

Thank You, Lord, for Your love and faithfulness. Thank You for making us Your people and for allowing us to be the sheep of Your pasture. Thank You for allowing us to serve such a great God!

293

Father God, the heroes that kids admire have weaknesses. Help young
souls to trust You as their only hero—the one they can trust forever and
ever. You are greater than any other, and You will always come through!

294

I know I can trust in You, Lord. Thank You for Your strength, which never fails.
It is there for all eternity. You don't weaken like I do. You are omnipotent.
All honor goes to You, for You alone are God. Amen.

295

Wonderful Counselor, help me to be receptive to Your voice and to always trust in
Your guidance. I especially need direction in the area of _____.

296

Lord, please create in me the fruit of self-control. Enable me to
walk in Your Spirit's power and to flee from temptation! Amen.

297

Lord, I want my heart to continually be filled with thanksgiving to You.
Keep me anchored in the thought that all You do is for my good.
Make my heart steadfast, and keep me from temptations.

298

Lord, thank You for being my best friend. You are kind, loving, generous, faithful, and giving. You always listen to me, and You have the best advice. But most of all, You laid down Your life for me—for me, Lord. Thank You!

299

Please help me to order my days so my priorities reflect Yours, Lord—so that I spend my time and energy as You would want me to. Amid the activity bombarding my life, center me on You. Teach me Christ-centered living so that wise choices will follow.

300

Lord, I pray that each successive generation will understand that all the glory for our many blessings belongs to You. Without You we would be nothing and would have nothing. May we praise Your name throughout the generations! Amen.

301

Alpha and Omega, beginning and end, from everlasting to everlasting You are God. Even though part of who You are is a mystery to me, I rest in the assurance that You, Jesus, are my Redeemer and friend. I will trust in You. Amen.

302

Father, I praise You for Your support. When my strength fails, Yours is always sufficient. Thank You for Your constant love and care, for knowing me by name, picking out my cry in the night, and never failing to rescue me.

303

Lord, help me to remember that although Your promises are free for the taking, I still need to accept them, claim them, and then live in faith that they are mine.

....

....

....

....

....

....

....

304

God, You have made everything beautiful. You have set eternity in my heart.
Lord, may I never sit in the gutter when the steps of paradise are at my feet!

305

I want to be a fruitful branch, Lord. With Your help I can, whether the fruit I
bring is a cheerful attitude or money to help provide for needs. Show me the
best way to contribute to the happiness of those around me. Amen.

306

Lord, I bring before You those who are in prison. Help them to know that You offer a
life of hope and peace. In their fear and loneliness, help them to find Your forgiveness,
joy, and light. Remind me to visit those in prison and fulfill Your commands.

307

Thank You, Father, for giving us sound doctrine. I have boundaries set by You
that I can follow. All I have to do is look to You and Your Word for guidance.
The boundaries You have established for me have fallen in pleasant places.

308

Lord, help me to soar free from the bounds of this sin-weary world. To imagine
beyond the ordinary. To love large. Forgive lavishly. Hope always. And to
expect a miracle. Father, give me a contagious enthusiasm for life in You!

309

Lord, thanks to You I get to start over, fresh and clean, because You have made
me a new person. I am forgiven and free in Christ Jesus. I now have a lifetime
of new days. Help me to spend each day bringing glory to You in some way.

310

Holy Spirit, I need deliverance from my anxiety. I know You are trustworthy.
I want to surrender my worries to You. Help me to trust You for all my needs.

311

Lord, I thank You for my coworkers. Please bless my relationships in the workplace.
Help me to put others above myself. Help us to work well as a team. Amen.

312

Lord, I have heartache in my soul. Please bring me comfort. Help me to learn to rest
in Your strong and loving arms. You are acquainted with grief, so You know my pain.

313

Lord, help me to use my spiritual gifts, those talents and abilities You've given
me to serve in the church and in ministries. Give me the heart of a servant.

314

God, please forgive me for my unkind thoughts about others. Help me to view
everyone with Your grace and love. Purify my mind and spirit with Your gentle touch.
Amen.

315

Lord God, You are truly awe-inspiring—full of mystery and majesty and marvelous
splendor. You alone are worthy of honor and glory! I praise Your holy name!

316

Thank You, Father God, that You reached down and saved me from myself. I was on the road to nowhere. Just as You did with Saul, You made Yourself known to me at just the right time. You've given me a new name. I'm a child of the living God!

317

One of the Ten Commandments tells us that the Lord's Day is more than a day of rest; it is also a holy day. So, let us worship You, Lord. Let us put up our feet. Let us be refreshed for a new week of loving and being loved. Amen.

318

Thank You, God, that even in Your discipline I discover Your mercy. Even when You allow me to struggle, there is joy!

319

Father, You are the origin of all richness, joy, and love. Help me to seek You every moment of every day. Amen.

320

Lord, some days—if I'm going to be truly honest—I feel like a total mess. Please work out the kinks in my very wrinkled character. Please refresh my spirit and help me to rely solely on Your guidance.

321

Father, help me to remember that—no matter how much a fellow human being may think and act like they have power over me—You have the ultimate authority, the utmost power, and the final say in my life. Praise God!

322

Lord, help me to make a home in the stronghold of Your love.
I don't want to rely on this world for my comfort or fulfillment.
You are my sustenance and my purpose. Amen.

323

Dearest Lord, when I suffer from an anxious heart or feel ensnared by this world with
no one to hear my cry for help, remind me that I can talk to You. Right now, I come.

324

I praise You, Lord, that the act of prayer is as simple as launching a boat into the Sea
of Galilee, and it's as miraculous as walking on water. Dear Lord, hear my prayer.

325

Jesus, help me to remember that my worth isn't defined by my outward appearance.
Transform me daily into a greater likeness of Yourself. Amen.

326

God, help me to trust in Your perfect plan, even when I don't understand it.
You are sovereign and all-knowing. I have no reason to fear because
You are in control. I place my life in Your hands. Right now.

327

Father, thank You for Your provision, hope, and joy. Without You,
life is dry and hostile. Come into my life and quench my thirst.
You are the only one who can fulfill me. Amen.

328

Lord, You are beautiful and without flaw, and I ask You to pour Your pure light into every dark crevice of this fallen earth—into every needy soul. I especially pray for _____.

329

Mighty Redeemer, help me to represent You and to light the way for others in this dark, fallen world. Thank You, Jesus, for Your mercy, love, and saving grace. Amen.

330

Almighty God, I know there is a war going on in the spiritual realms, and it's a fight like no other. You are my strength and protection. Defend me from evil, unseen forces. Amen.

331

Holy Spirit, give me new eyes so that I can see others as You see them. Help me to love as You love—without selfishness or limit. Amen.

332

Heavenly Father, help me to be always mindful of my eternal home and to spread the boundless joy and peace that comes from that hope. Amen.

333

Jesus, may I never forget the power of Your sacrifice on the cross! Let me allow You to remove the rubbish of my past sins, once and for all, and rejoice in a clean heart. Amen.

....

....

....

....

....

....

....

....

334

Lord, I want to always be ready to open that bottle of reconciliation and let its pleasing scent flow into my heart—and then onto my lips. God, please give me a humble heart so that I can make amends and let go of grudges.

335

I thank You, Jesus, for casting away my sin as far as the east is from the west and remembering it no more! What freedom. What joy!

336

Sweet Savior, thank You for enduring the pain of the cross and for taking on my sin so that I can enjoy all of eternity with You. Amen.

337

God, help me to accept others as You accepted me. Guide and sustain me as I extend Your love and grace to the world.

338

My Redeemer, help me to rely fully on Your grace, provision, and love. Thank You for being steadfast and always present. Just as You are now.

339

Lord Jesus, I know we have every reason to light up with excitement and wonder on Easter morning. We should be bursting with enthusiasm, unable to contain our joy. After all, we have the best surprise and hope of all. We have an empty tomb! Praise Your holy name!

340

Every beat of my heart and breath I take is from Your merciful hand.
Thank You for this amazing gift called life! Amen.

341

Awesome God, You are the author of all creation and truly worthy to
be praised. Make a home in my heart so that my every thought, action,
and word will reflect Your wonderful character. Thank You for allowing
me to have such a close, intimate connection with You. Amen.

342

Lord Jesus, sometimes I feel unloved and unappreciated. Please remind
me how I am treasured in Your sight. How much You love me.
And how You pursue me more diligently than a lover. Amen.

343

Holy Spirit, please let me see what You see, and let me be courageous
enough to follow through with Your divine appointments—ones that
could change a life. Whom would You have me talk to today?

344

Father, on hard days, help me not to doubt and grumble and fuss like a
small child. I can be such a whiner! Help me to love You with all my
heart, soul, and strength in every circumstance—good or bad. Amen.

345

My Lord and Savior, thank You for the promise that Your love will follow me
all the days of my life and I will live in Your house forever. I have good reason
to share this good news, to shout this joy, and to celebrate this victory!

346

Almighty God, You are marvelous. You are beautiful. You are the Kings of
kings and Lord of lords. With You, Jesus, every day is a hallelujah moment!

347

Lord, sometimes I come down with a bad case of the "what if" blues.
During these times, please stay near me and give me Your strength,
Your comfort, and Your peace. Amen.

348

God, I'm so grateful that You can turn evil into good and sorrow into joy.
I need You now, especially concerning _____.

349

In obtaining wisdom, Lord, I know that the asking and the receiving are only
a prayer away. Please give me the wisdom I need in order to live a life that is
pleasing to You. I particularly need wise counsel in the area of _____.

350

Father, You are my greatest treasure, my deepest joy, and my brightest hope.
I delight in Your presence. Life can't get much better than that.

351

God, how wonderful it is that You hear me when I call out to You and that You
answer with exactly what I need. I come to You now with my burdens.

....

....

....

....

....

....

....

....

....

352

Mighty King, Your glory and majesty are beyond compare.
Help me to worship You all the days of my life. Amen.

353

Lord, help me to have the courage to offer Your message of good news to
this weary and heartbroken world. I especially pray for _____.

354

Holy Spirit, I know it only takes a moment to change a life—to be a blessing. Please
be the voice in my ear that inclines me to do good and to love much. Amen.

355

Thank You, Lord, that You are not a god who can be easily contained or controlled
or categorized. We need a God who is like You—the Lion of Judah. Creator God,
I am in awe of Your vastness, wisdom, and mystery! Hallelujah!

356

Dear God, You have put a song in my heart that needs singing. You have given
me a new day for rejoicing. You have given me good news to shout. What
miracles and blessings do You want me to share with the world today?

357

Gracious God, remind me that there will be no striving in heaven for material gain
and glory, since we'll be able to see it for what it is—fleeting and fluttery like a
butterfly, but not nearly as beautiful. In You alone I find true contentment. Amen.

358

Thank You, Jesus, that You care for me. I know You may not sweep away all the trials from this life, but I know You will be near me. You will never fail me, and You'll bring good out of all I endure. Praise Your holy name!

359

Holy Spirit, help me to hear Your voice clearly and follow its sound when so many others are shouting. Help me to grow and become what You made me to be in the body of Christ. Amen.

360

Thank You, Lord, for the promise that one day You will take me to live with You, where there will be no more pain or hunger or tears or disease or war or disasters. Only light, love, and joy. But until heaven, help me to trust and rest in You.

361

Almighty God, help me always remember that every word I say has consequences. Help me not to lose control of my tongue! Remind me instead to speak words of life and love and truth and joy. Amen.

362

Great Physician, remind me to put my trust in Your perfectly capable hands, and help me to see all the many ways You heal me, over and over again. I am especially grateful for _____.

363

God, when amazing things happen to me, help me to remember to give You the glory first before I open my mouth to tell the story. Help me to value what You have to say to me more than the sound of my own voice. Amen.

364

Lord, remind me to help my fellow sojourners. Please help me not to be a bump in anyone's road but instead to point the way to You and Your message of salvation. Amen.

365

Oh God, please bring my attention to the times when I get prideful. Help me to remember that there is no facet of arrogance that looks pretty from heaven. Or on earth.

366

Yes, the prudent "hold their tongues" (Proverbs 10:19). Lord, please remind me that if I make wise choices when it comes to what I say, I won't have so much damage control later. Help my choices to be wiser, and my words more worthwhile. Amen.

367

The fear of the Lord is beautiful and enlightening and exciting and challenging and good. And that's a great place to start. God, help me to always start with You.

368

Dear God, You know our hearts and the worries that prey on our minds.
Please help us to stay busy doing good and to grow in trust and patience.
Please help us to let go of the control we never had to start with. Amen.

369

My God, my friend, my lover, my Savior. Humble me, so You can lift me up. Amen.

370

Dear God, let me be an instrument of Your peace. Help me, in whatever conversations
or relationships I develop, to build up unity among Your followers. Amen.

371

Lord, help me to be keenly aware of all that I do in this world.
That I am genuinely doing good, and not just doing. Amen.

372

Thank You, Lord, for Your amazing mercy and grace and for vanquishing the lies
of the deceiver. With Your supernatural help I am able to live a life of victory!

373

Lord Jesus, help me to realize the value of my heart
and to treat it as the precious thing it is. Amen.

374

Dear God, help me not to worry about what I don't have but to be content with what I do have. Help me to be grateful for everything. I especially thank You for

_____.

375

Dear Lord, help me to study Your Word and take it to heart so I can pass it on. Amen.

376

There is no victory so sweet as that which comes through steadfast surrender to the God who watches us all. Help me, Lord, to always follow You with abandon.

377

Father, help me to be compassionate and winsome in the way I share my testimony. I want to be the kind of person who can shed Your light and love on others. Amen.

378

Father, may my love for You be steadfast and my worship of You be genuine, constant, and contagious to all who cross my path!

379

Dear Jesus, thank You that I am safe in Your dwelling place, hidden in the shelter of Your arms. I am grateful for Your boundless protection and provision in my darkest hours. Amen.

....

....

....

....

....

....

....

....

380

Lord, help me to have the energy and spirit to do what is good for
Your kingdom. And when I am tired, please refresh my soul!

381

Dear Jesus, thank You for giving me the strength to endure any situation.
Thank You for supplying what I need so I don't ever have to worry. Amen.

382

Lord of all, thank You for always challenging me
to be a better me. Help me make You proud!

383

Lord, help me to spend time, not chasing shadows, but looking to Your
glorious radiance. Thank You for being the Light of the world! Amen.

384

Lord, hear me when I am sad and feel alone. Show me that You are with
me and that my grief will not go on forever. Please be near me as I pray.

385

Dear Provider of everything we need and everything we enjoy, help me not to be so
concerned about worldly things but to cling to things that are eternal. Amen.

386

Dear God, You knew what would happen when You let Your Son
into this world. And You still let Him go. What a sacrifice of love!
Dear Father, let me live a life worthy of Your love. Amen.

387

Lord, instead of me working hard to get everything just right,
please allow Your Holy Spirit to do His work in me. Instead of
me desiring my idea of perfection, help me to desire to please You.

388

Laughter can be a beautiful, powerful thing. And it's wonderful to have
a God who laughs with me. Dear God, help me to laugh more.

389

Over and over again, Lord, You show me that You care for me. And over and
over again, You reveal that You want to be with me, to fellowship with me,
even in my mess. Thank You, Lord, for loving me so consistently. Amen.

390

Dear God, please forgive me for my mistakes. Please help me to let Your power
be strong in me. I especially need help when it comes to _____.

391

Lord, I know that in order to defeat the devil's schemes of distraction I will need to
focus on truth, righteousness, gospel readiness, faith, salvation, the Word of God,
and prayer. Dear mighty God, help me be fit for the real battle at hand. Amen.

392

Oh Lord, I don't want to be a foolhardy and stubborn character in the story of this broken world. I need to be honest about _____. Please forgive me and send me Your peace. Amen.

393

Lord Jesus, please help me to stop doing wrong. Help me to learn to do what is right and good in Your sight. Let me be clean, bright, pure, and simple. Like the falling snow.

394

Oh Lord God, remember me in my suffering. When the rains come, when sorrow floods my soul, when my mountains crumble, please remember me. God, help me to always place my hope in You. Amen.

395

Dear Lord, please remind me that anytime and every time I replace You with something else—food, money, sex, fame, drugs— I will lose out. Help me to always be satisfied by You. Amen.

396

Lord, I know You can see inside me, past my fronts and disguises. You can see through my actions and know my heart. Since You know everything about me, it's clear to see I desperately need You. Please help me, especially in the area of _____.

397

Dear Lord, help me to give as much grace to others as You have given me. Amen.

....

....

....

....

....

....

....

398

Lord Jesus, I know You don't want words from me that mean nothing
or promises that don't go anywhere. I know You need obedience.
Help me to submit to You in all areas of my life. Amen.

399

Dear God, I am an unorganized mess, and I feel as though I don't have
time for anything important. Please help me to be a better manager
of my time, and help me balance my priorities. Amen.

400

Dear God, I admit that sometimes I get nervous and feel a need to fill
the air with too many words. And sometimes that "talk" turns
into a bit of gossip. Please help me to guard my words.

401

Lord, help me to remember that it is far better to rain down compliments rather
than complaints and to provide refreshment to those around me instead of a
roomful of hot air! Please let Your sweet Spirit rain down on me now.

402

Oh Lord, my God, help me listen for Your song, and help
me find the words to sing praise to You every day. Amen.

403

Lord, I know that when I live a wise life, people take notice. And that can be a
beautiful thing. Please bless me with wisdom every day so I can honor You. Amen.

....

....

....

....

....

....

....

404

Holy Spirit, help me not to be so mesmerized by the charms of
this world that I forget what are lies and what is truth. Amen.

405

Dear almighty God, help me to rely on what is true and right for
all time, instead of what seems good for the moment. Amen.

406

I am facing a battle, and I can't do this on my own. Almighty God,
I know You are all-powerful, all-knowing, all-mighty, and all-good.
Please be my guide, my leader, and my defender. Amen.

407

Lord, I can sense Your presence around me. I can hear Your whispers of love.
Oh Lord, my God, thank You for the beautiful mystery of You. Amen.

408

Dear Lord, help me not to take pride in owning things, nor become afraid of losing
what I own, but to simply have a grateful heart and put my trust in You. Amen.

409

Lord Jesus, thank You for loving me as I am but also for loving
me enough to make me into a better Christian. I want to
become every wonderful thing You created me to be.

410

What kind of Christmas would it be if there weren't still some mystery? I praise You, Lord, for everything You are—the parts I know, and the parts I don't.

411

Lord, this world is full of people who tell falsehoods and cheat and don't keep their vows. Help me to believe in You and all the promises in Your Word, even when things don't go my way. Amen.

412

When people mourn, Lord, help me to learn how to be still and listen. To learn about what the other person needs. Please give me a greater gift of empathy so I can serve others well. Amen.

413

Lord, please help me to be a trustworthy person. I want to labor in such a way that no one has to check my work. I desire to be a good manager of my time and resources. To act with honesty and integrity. Amen.

414

Thank You, Lord, that Your Word is so powerful and so penetrating that we could post a warning sign on the church door—BEWARE: THE WORD OF GOD MIGHT CHANGE YOUR LIFE! Dear God, I praise You for the gift of Your Word.

415

Dear Jesus, thank You for being a friend that I can always trust. And when I give You all my worries, please help me not to snatch them back five minutes later. Show me how to leave those fears and burdens in Your capable hands instead. Amen.

416

I refuse to be discouraged by this world. I know that the same Jesus who rebuked the devil in the desert is walking with me every step of the way in my wilderness. Thank You, Lord, for keeping my heart safe.

417

Lord Jesus, too often I say what I want when I want—and my remarks are voiced without a kind and gentle spirit. Please help me to shape this sharp tongue of mine into an instrument of peace. Amen.

418

Dear God, thank You for providing for me. Help me to rely on You daily for everything I need. Amen.

419

Thank You, Lord, for the wisdom of scholars and the guidance of good teachers. Help me to find both when I need them so I can learn about Your Word. Amen.

420

Lord, Christ, I desire to renew my mind in You. I want to come closer to living like the person You created me to be. Let me be a daily, living sacrifice.

421

Dear Author of my life, help me to remember to trust You to write my story. Amen.

....

....

....

....

....

....

....

....

422

Sometimes it is right to be quiet. Dear God, help me to be wise about when to speak up and when to offer people the gift of silence. Amen.

423

Dear God—my King, my life, my light—help me to know for certain who I am and to find all my confidence in You. Amen.

424

Dear Lord, bless the work of my hands and feet. Make me Your servant so that, at the end of my life, I can look forward to hearing You say, "Well done." Amen.

425

God, thank You for the steady anchor of the church and the opportunity to fellowship with a vibrant community of believers. I particularly want to pray for _____.

426

Help me, Lord, to stay prayerfully focused on You and Your way for me, and then the peace that passes all understanding will not be a distant mirage but authentic. Amen.

427

God, impress on my mind and heart that serving is not insignificant or pointless, but it has infinite, eternal worth. Amen.

428

Thank You, Lord, that You are not a dead prophet but the risen King.
And when people ask, "What do you see in Him?" I will say,
"Christ is my Savior." I praise You for Your saving grace!

429

Lord Jesus, You took the concept of servanthood to the
most profound depth and yet to the highest height of all.
Thank You for this incredible sacrifice! Praise Your holy name!

430

Lord, help me to remember that this self-centered, prideful mode of mine only leads
to more wear and tear on my spirit. Let me make life simple again. To trust fully.
Submit willingly. I especially need guidance in the area of _____.

431

Lord, someone has been insensitive toward me. Please don't let it ruin my day, and
help me not to respond with a curt remark or thoughts of revenge. Let me choose
patience. Show me how to turn the other cheek. Help me to choose love.

432

God, help me to be persistent in prayer even when I can't see the direct fruits of it.
Don't let me give up on the power of prayer. Amen.

433

Please, Lord, help me not to let the sun go down on my anger.
I don't want to let bad feelings fester, so help me to be
quick in saying I'm sorry when I need to. Amen.

434

On the days I feel deprived, Lord, help me to slow down and think of all that others are lacking—and what I can do about it. If there is someone who needs an encouraging word or a helping hand, please bring that person to mind right now.

435

Dear God, help me make wise choices so that the way
I live my life may bring glory to You and hope to others.

436

God, help me be patient with my brothers and sisters in Christ. Help me to overlook offenses and forgive quickly. Help me to see them as Your children. Amen.

437

Lord, I know that a broken heart will never be the same. It is forever scarred.
But with the scarring comes wisdom, and that wisdom can blossom into
compassion for others who have been hurt as well. Help me to
use that compassion for Your holy purposes. Amen.

438

Dear God, help me to be humble, knowing all
the wisdom I have comes from You. Amen.

439

God, You brought all life into existence. You are glorious
beyond measure. Help me to grasp the magnitude of
Your brilliance and to give praise from a sincere heart!

440

Lord, help me to remember that while dreams and goals can be good,
if I let ambition become all about me, it won't be worth much
at the end of the day or the end of a life. Amen.

441

In the end, Lord, remind me what matters most.
That I knew You as my God, my friend, my Redeemer.

442

Jesus, through Your power and kindness, instruct me
in the ways of wisdom that come from heaven. Amen.

443

God, don't allow me to distract myself with petty, frivolous things, but help me
instead to live my life for Your glory with a gentle, willing spirit. Amen.

444

Holy Spirit, please break down the walls around my heart and sweep out the dusty,
dark places that harbor sin, bitterness, and distrust. Please help me now.

445

Oh Lord, my Rock, thank You for the safety and strength You provide.
Shield me from temptation, and help me to cling to Your beautiful promises.

446

Lord, thank You that You are the strength in my branches, the wisdom
in my spirit, and the light that gives me life! Praise Your holy name!

447

Lord, may Your light be present in every facet of my life. Help me to
avoid any worldly customs that could be harmful to my witness. Amen.

448

Holy Spirit, guide me in my decisions. Help me to be wise, clearheaded,
and motivated by a selfless love for You and others. Amen.

449

Lord, help me avoid the temptation of airing my good deeds to the masses.
May they be done for Your eyes and Your glory only. Amen.

450

Lord, remind me daily that wise words can bring healing. They wear well—
like a string of fine pearls that will not break. Costly. Strong. Beautiful.
Wise words can be repeated without fear or regret. No apology will
be necessary. What wise words do You have for me today?

451

Lord, help me spread the seeds of generosity among friends and strangers.
Thank You for the joy and renewal that giving freely to others provides.
Whom can I bless today with my generosity?

452

Father, give me a discerning spirit when I'm confronted with entertainment that might pollute my mind and spirit with things that displease You. Amen.

453

Lord, I can be such a doubting Thomas at times! It's like being tossed to and fro on stormy waves. When life's circumstances or the Enemy of my soul try to tempt me with doubts about You, please calm that sea of fear and those terrible waves of disbelief.

454

Thank You, God, that You always listen to my prayers, and You always answer. It may not be the reply I want, but praise You that it will always be an answer from the vantage point of omnipotence and not human frailty!

455

God, give me patience in times of frustration and gentle words for everyone I meet. Be present in my every action. Amen.

456

Lord, thank You for Your intervention on my behalf— even when my faith is only the size of a mustard seed.

457

Heavenly Father, help me to exhibit a pure, selfless love and to resist the urge to correct and criticize. May my presence be a soothing balm for everyone I encounter. Amen.

....

....

....

....

....

....

....

458
Jesus, thank You for the peace and joy You offer to those
who follow You. I was created to love and be loved by You.

459
Sweet Savior, don't allow the hopelessness of this world to
discourage me. I choose to believe in Your saving power. Amen.

460
Oh Lord, shine Your light into every corner of my heart.
My spirit may at first squint at the sudden bright light,
but I will also rest in the joy that comes from a clean heart!

461
Lord, remind me to listen more and talk less. To not make my point
so sharp that it jabs at someone's heart! God, give me restraint and
consideration when I interact with friends, family, and strangers. Amen.

462
Lord, help me remain faithful to all Your commandments,
even the ones that seem small or inconsequential at the time. Amen.

463
God, give me the wisdom to see any snares set by Satan,
and please give me the strength to resist these temptations. Amen.

....

....

....

....

....

....

....

....

464

Help me to reach out to lessen someone else's lonesomeness, Lord,
and in that kind deed, perhaps I will ease my own. Deepen and enrich my
relationships with family and friends, especially with _____.

465

Holy Spirit, convict me when I'm showing partiality in a desperate,
selfish attempt to feel included and important. I want to live life by Your
standards, seeing through the exterior and straight into the heart. Amen.

466

Lord, help me not to be a slave to perfectionism,
but in all things, let me find balance and joy. Amen.

467

God, I know I'm not meant to stumble on sin but glide in Your grace! Lord, thank
You that You have a plan for me, a hope and a future. Show me the way—Your way.

468

Thank You, Lord Jesus, that even while I was deep in my sin, You gave
up Your life so that I might truly live. What a sacrifice. What a Savior!
Thank You for Your unfathomable mercy, Your immeasurable love. Amen.

469

Creator God, help me to grasp the beautiful simplicity of prayer.
I want an unceasing, rich communion with You, my Lord and Savior. Amen.

470

Lord, I know in my heart that You are the answer that I've always searched for.
I can't resist Your ways or the love in Your eyes a moment longer.

471

God, may I strive to know You as You really are, not as I want You to be.
May I never limit Your power in my life, for You are a holy and
awesome God of infinite power and might! Amen.

472

Dear Healer, mend the holes in my heart
so I can offer my whole heart to You.

473

Lord, help me to always denounce the destructive lies of the thief, Satan.
Show me how to embrace the truth of Christ and live a free and abundant
life. I want to be all the beautiful things You intended me to be!

474

Oh Lord, search my heart and find the brokenness. Then carefully over time,
please join the pieces together—with new love, care, and understanding.

475

Dear Lord, help me to keep my temper when I'm under attack.
Help me to be patient. Help me to choose glory. Amen.

476

Dear Lord, catch me in my pride, and help
me consider my actions carefully. Amen.

477

Dearest Lord, clothe me with an attitude of selflessness and humility.
Help me to live a life that blesses the people around me. Amen.

478

Lord, give me a heart of compassion. Show me how to smile even when I want to
frown. Show me how to be handier with a cup of cool water than a witty comeback.
Teach me how to chase after a lost soul faster than I chase after a good time.

479

Jesus, help me to grow strong in the rich,
nourishing soil of Your love and grace.

480

God, remind me of the weight of my words, and help me to refrain
from speaking carelessly. Give me encouraging, compassionate words
instead of words that could cause pain or anger. Amen.

481

Jesus, I give You my doubts, fears, and insecurities.
Thank You for hearing all my prayers—great and small.

482

Holy Spirit, help me to fly free of my past and become
the person of wisdom You intended me to be. Amen.

483

Lord, help me not to only pray when I want something.
That is, begging for a finer job, better health, and a bigger
house. Please help me love You as a real friend. Amen.

484

Jesus, I want to be daily reminded of the pricelessness of Your
gift of grace. Thank You for all You have done and continue
to do. I particularly want to thank You for _____.

485

Lord, when I am feeling anxious, help me to remember that
You hold me in the palm of Your hand. You have the
power to restore and refresh my weary soul. Amen.

486

Dear Lord, please use the turbulent times in my life to help make me
beautiful in my spirit. I want to glorify You and be all that You created me to be.

487

Oh Lord, I want to rejoice in all the good things that You
have given me. Thank You for all the beauty, joy, and splendor
that life has to offer. Please cultivate in me a grateful spirit. Amen.

488

You are truly incredible and awesome and glorious! Lord God, help me to comprehend Your magnitude and glory. I want to be awestruck by You.

489

Father, please take away my heavy burdens. Just as a child trusts an earthly father, help me to trust You with every aspect of my life. I give it all to You right now.

490

Father, please be present in my heart and thoughts always. Never let our communion and fellowship be severed. I want every area of my life to be committed to You through sincere, continual prayer. Amen.

491

Lord, give me a spirit of humility and sincerity when I pray in front of others. Help me to remember that prayer should not be used to show others how godly and well spoken I am, but to connect with You, the living God.

492

Lord, You have the power to guide and restore nations. Please help the people of this country to humble themselves and acknowledge their sin and their need for You. Amen.

493

God, thank You for hearing my prayers. For watching over my comings and goings. For loving me, infusing me with hope, and giving me life eternal! Amen.

....

....

....

....

....

....

....

....

494
Jesus, help me to follow You with boldness, joy, and trust.
I want to see life through heaven-bound eyes. Be my everything.

495
Holy Spirit, don't ever let me lose hope. You are my protector, provider,
and comforter. Even when I feel desperately alone and downtrodden,
help me to remember that You are always there for me. Just as You are now.

496
Father, thank You for taking what is miserable and tragic and working it for good
through Your power and sovereignty. Help me to trust in Your promises.

497
God, give me the strength and patience to encounter the world with
the abounding love of Christ. Help me to love as You love. Amen.

498
Lord, there are many times when I need You and Your Word to
guide me. Lead me, and help me become an overcomer. Amen.

499
Father, You have given me Your Word and Your Holy Spirit to
teach me. Help me to seek You each day, and help me to listen.

500

Lord, mold and shape me into a brilliant display of Your likeness.
I want to reflect the many facets of Your character to those I encounter.
Make me malleable to Your touch and receptive to Your voice.

501

Father, thank You for all You have given me, for all You have
taught me, and for all the good times still to come. Amen.

502

Lord, my mind wanders today. I find myself thinking of past sorrows
and old wounds. Please bring me peace. Help me remember that
forgiveness and healing come from You. Let me recall all the ways
You have brought me joy and mended my broken heart.

503

God, the source of all hope and the only true hope, let me fight against anxiety this
hour with the knowledge of Your faithful promises. I want to glimpse the reality of
heaven—where there will be no more crying or mourning or pain or sickness.

504

God, I heard a troubling story in the news today. There is so much suffering
in the world. I can't bear the weight of it on my own. Please take these
burdens from me and put in my hands some good work I can do.

505

Father, I want to be a child—no bills to pay, no hard work to do. But I know
I cannot run away. Help me to find joy in my responsibilities. Help me be
grateful for honest work. Help me rejoice in one more day to know You more.

....

....

....

....

....

....

506

Lord, You are so kind and good to me. I can't understand Your generous grace,
but I love it! I love the way You take my wrongs and lift them away.
It feels so good—the sweet joy of a heart washed clean.

507

God, it's a gray and dreary day outside, and all I want to do is sleep.
Help me to get out of my bed. Help me to move my feet. Help me to keep
my hands busy. Help me to find motivation. Help me to just keep going.

508

God, I bit into an apple today and was delighted with its juicy sweetness.
And then I thought—every good and perfect thing is from You! Even this delicious
apple! And I just wanted to say thank You for providing for us so well.

509

God, give me courage. I must tell someone I love something that is hard to say. I need
to be truthful, but it's so hard, God. Please give me the right words. Help me not to
say things in a way that will hurt but to say them in a way that will help.

510

God, today I'm just not feeling it. That's all. And I don't know why. Can You help?
Can You show me a reason to try? Can You tell me why it all matters? I'm going
to go to Your Word, Lord. Help me hear what You have to say.

511

Oh Lord, today is going to be a long one. I have so much to do; I don't even know where to start. Help me make a good beginning. Give me energy to keep going every hour. And at the end of the day, let me remember to thank You.

512

Lord, draw near to me. And may that intimate fellowship between us reflect in my countenance, in my actions, and in my every word. Amen.

513

Lord, sometimes I just don't understand people. I can't comprehend why they do the things they do—why people hurt others. God, help me not to just shut down and shut out the world. That seems easy to do. Help me try to understand others instead.

514

God, I messed up today. I deceived someone. Please forgive me. Please help me have the courage to tell the truth. Please lead me to examine my life and get rid of everything that doesn't bring me closer to You. Lead me now.

515

Father, I heard about someone who is going through a lot of pain. I feel awkward reaching out. I don't know how to help. What can I do? Help me to see.

516

Jesus, I know You'll understand. You know what it is to be tempted. You know what it's like to walk on this earth and feel the weight of its darkness. Please give me Your strength. Please help me to walk in the light.

517

Lord, I want Your living water. I want the water that never
dries up, never flows away, and never destroys. My soul needs
Your refreshment. Please fill me up with Your Spirit.

518

God, You know what I'm going through. It helps me to talk to You about it.
But I know I need to talk to someone else too. I just don't know how.
Let's face it, I'm scared. Please give me the courage to speak. I need help.

519

God, the world is moving so fast! I think about all the changes I've seen in
my lifetime and it's amazing. Sometimes I just want to make time stand
still. Lord God, help us not to lose sight of You in the blur of our days.

520

What's happening, God? People are so divided. People are lashing out at each
other. And sometimes I get caught up in the fight. Please help me to know
Your peace. Please help me to speak Your peace. Please help me.

521

God, You created so many amazing works of art—the mountains piercing
the blue sky, the rivers cutting through the forests, the ocean waves
crashing on the shores. I stand in awe of Your never-ending creativity.
I pray I can make something beautiful happen today.

522

Sometimes, God, I don't even understand myself. I'm surprised by my emotions. I'm confused by my inability to stick to my decisions. I'm puzzled by my relationships. Can You help me figure things out?

523

God, You know what I want most of all right now. I've been wanting it for so long. You know what I would sacrifice to get it. Grant me patience. I know Your timing is perfect and Your plans are so much wiser than mine. Help me to wait.

524

Jesus, I don't know how You did it. You faced all those people who hated You and You died for them. You gave everything. I feel like I can't even give my enemies a smile— much less make any real sacrifice. Help me understand how to love them.

525

Lord, I heard a siren passing just now, and I am reminded of all those who are facing a crisis. How many must happen each day? And yet You see them all. You are there for them all. God, help those who need emergency intervention.

526

God, I don't know why this is happening. I feel so lost. I've been rejected and it hurts. But I know I can depend on You. I know You will never leave me. I know You can fill up this hole inside me. Help me be filled.

527

Lord Almighty, I know some people who need Your power. They need to know that they are in Your hands. They need to feel safe. They need to know the love that will not let them go. I lift up their names to You.

528

Lord, I wonder sometimes how often You just look at us, Your creations, and shake Your head. How ridiculous our efforts to control things must look to You! God, I tried to control my life this week and it didn't go so well. Here's what happened. . . .

529

God, I'm holding on to so many secrets. I don't know what to do with them all. People confide in me. They come to me for help. But I don't know how to help them all. God, please lead me in Your wisdom. Give me discernment.

530

God, I am filled with Your joy! Thank You for putting me at just this time and just this place! I don't know what tomorrow will bring, but today I rejoice in Your plan, and I thank You for making me part of it.

531

God, I flip a switch and a light comes on. I wish it were that easy to find my own energy. I wish I could just flip a switch and feel Your power flowing through me. Lord, help this body do what it needs to do today.

532

God, I was reading about the amazing ways You showed Yourself to the Israelites—in a pillar of fire, in thunder on the mountain, in the flames of a bush. I'm glad I don't have to climb a mountain to hear You speak to me.

....

....

....

....

....

....

....

....

....

533

Jesus, I'm overwhelmed with gratitude for what You've done for me.
I don't understand why You did it—I can't fathom that kind of love.
Help me to live a life that shows my thanks. Help me start right now.

534

Lord, I know You've given us Your Spirit. I have felt Your comfort, and I have leaned
on Your help. But right now I need Your guidance. I've got some hard choices to
make. Please help me. And help me have the courage to do Your will.

535

Lord, I'm so thankful for Your Word. It's amazing how often I look in it and feel
like You are speaking straight to me. Help me remember that when I don't know
where else to go, I can come to Your Word and find exactly what I need.

536

God, wake me up. I feel like I've been floating along, just cruising through
life and not really participating. The worst part is I don't know how to
change. Show me one thing I can do today to make a difference.

537

Father God, I have little eyes watching me. I know the children in my life
need someone to show them how to make good choices and live right.
I'm afraid I'm not always the best example for them. Help me to do better.

538

God, today I'm thankful for things that make me smile. A silly puppy, a bird singing its heart out, a parking space right by the front door. Thanks for knowing when I need to be cheered up. You always seem to know exactly what I need.

539

Lord, I know I'm not the most popular person in my little world right now. I've had to make some tough decisions. I understand why people aren't happy with me, but it still hurts. Help me to know what to do next.

540

God, You spoke and there was light. You shaped the earth. You breathed life into man. You conquered death. I cannot even begin to measure Your might. I cannot even begin to picture that kind of power. Wow!

541

Lord, can I just take a break sometimes? Is it okay to stop being so good every once in a while? Would it really cause that much trouble? Yes, okay. I remember what's happened in the past. I will try not to grow weary of doing good.

542

God, I have many good memories, but sometimes it seems the sad and painful ones throw shadows on all the others. Help me to cling to the good in my life and to shine Your light in the shadows.

543

I was noticing the grain in the planks of a wood floor today, Lord. The pattern of every piece was different, yet all of them together looked so beautiful. Help me to see people that way, Lord. Help me to see how, together, we can be beautiful.

544

God, where do all the missing socks go? Why can no one ever put a new roll of toilet paper out? Why do I always lose my keys right when it's time to go? These are the mysteries on my mind. Thanks for listening, even to my smallest problems.

545

God, I've failed. I tried. I feel like I really tried. But I have failed again. And it hurts so much. But even worse, it has hurt others—the people I love most in the world. Help me figure out how to ask for forgiveness. I am depending on You.

546

God, this world needs Your love so much. And I feel like such a weak substitute to show it to them. But help me do what I can, whenever I can, wherever I go.

547

Jesus, I want to know You more. I read Your story laid out in the Gospels, and I just have so many questions about You. Help me to keep learning. Help me to keep seeking You. Help me to be a good friend to You.

548

Lord, my heart is a strange thing. I don't understand it. Does anyone? It wants things sometimes that I know are not good. Yet the desire is so strong. Help me to know how to overcome this longing and fill my heart with Your love.

549

God, I've had a setback. It's not so big, I guess, by some standards. But it feels big to me. I'm finding it hard to keep on the path that You've set for me. Please help me keep my feet moving on the road that leads to You.

550

God, I've met a lot of people in my life, but I've never met someone as difficult as _____. I know You've dealt with a lot of hard hearts, Lord. Help me figure out how to love this one.

551

Lord, this world is bigger than I can even understand. There are so many places I haven't seen, so many cultures I know nothing about. Help me not to make judgments about people that I don't know. Help me to see every person as Your child.

552

God, sometimes I feel so numb. I know I should care about others. I know I should mourn when they mourn and hurt when they hurt. But I just can't feel it. Help my compassion to grow. What can I do to have a heart like Yours?

553

Lord, people say to be careful what you wish for, and I feel like I've learned that lesson just now. I've got trouble on my hands, and I know I've made it for myself. I'm sorry, Lord. I should have listened to You. Will You help me?

554

God, my body is failing, but my heart is going strong. I want to laugh. I want to talk. I want to meet new people and see new things. Help me overcome frustration when my body won't let me do everything I want to do. Help me rejoice in the possible.

555

God, I know what it's like to have nothing, and I know what it's like to have a lot. Help me share what I have. Help me be content, knowing You have always provided for me. Help me remember what You have given.

556

Sometimes, Lord, I get caught up in scratching out a life for myself. I get so tangled up in my big plans, I forget that You drew the blueprints. Help me to go back to where I started. Help me to depend on You.

557

Lord, I want to list some things that You have done for me. I know You know all about them, Lord, but I need to remember. Please jog my memory, clear my mind, and help me think about the good You have brought to my life.

558

Jesus, I'm so thankful that You came to earth. It wasn't for long, and I know we don't have all the words You said, but I'm so grateful for what we do have. I'm so happy to know a God who would walk with us.

559

God, I saw someone come to know You today, and it was a beautiful thing. Please be with _____. The acceptance has come, but there is a hard road ahead. Help me to be an encouragement to those who are just beginning to walk with You.

560

Lord, You give such good gifts to Your children! Please
help me give good gifts to others. Help me give wisdom,
understanding, kindness, patience, and time. Help me give love.

561

Lord, I want to serve as Your hands and feet. Show me how my gifts line up with the
work that needs to be done in Your kingdom. Give me a humble heart so I may
serve others with no thought of receiving thanks or honor. Let me glorify You.

562

Oh Lord, I am so full of worries. At night I toss and turn, thinking of present
problems I can't solve and troubles that haven't even happened yet.
Calm my heart, Lord. Soothe my soul. Quiet my mind.

563

Jesus, You always spoke with such grace and authority. I want to be a good witness for
You, but my words come slowly. I don't feel like I know enough to answer anyone's
questions. Help me to find my voice, Lord. Grant me wisdom and understanding.

564

Father God, I need some advice. Help me rest in Your Word
today. Guide me to the stories that will speak to my problem.
Lead me to the peace that can only be found in You.

565

God, thank You. I don't know why You are so good to me. I don't deserve Your generosity. Your grace is overwhelming. I bow before You, King of kings. I give You my worship. I give You my heart. I give You this day.

566

God, my tongue has got in the way once again. I spoke in haste. I said too much. And I can't take back my words. Please mend the brokenness I have created. Please heal the wounds I have opened. Please help me know how to begin to say I'm sorry.

567

God, I long to live in Your glorious heaven. I can't even imagine a place where there is no sound of suffering—where no one cries out in hunger, where no one moans with aches, where no one gasps for breath. I can't wait to live there.

568

Days come and go, Lord, and we keep making plans. We keep filling up our calendars with things to do. I know I haven't made enough space for You in my life lately, Lord. Help me to fix that.

569

Jesus, how did You deal with Your enemies with such grace? I know You must have felt anger sometimes. Yet You didn't offer insults. You didn't lash out. You didn't cause harm. You just kept speaking the same message. Help me to stick to that message too.

570

God, remind me that success sometimes looks like failure, that closeness sometimes requires conflict, and that real relationships are almost always messy. Remind me, Lord, and let me be grateful for the life I have.

571

God, Your work in my life feels painful at times. I know You are making all things new. Help me to trust You more. Help me not to miss the old me. Help me to keep hanging on!

572

Lord, I need to remember that You are bigger than my bad day. You go deeper than I will ever fall. You go farther than I can run. You are before me and behind me, above me and below me. And I will follow You!

573

God, I hear You asking me to watch and pray. And I have to say, my spirit isn't even that willing right now, and my flesh is certainly weak (Matthew 26:41). So I will rely on Your Spirit, and I will lean on the body of Christ.

574

God, I want to pray for my friend, _____. You know the challenge ahead. You know the strength that will be needed to make it through this trial. You know just what is at stake. Please bring Your comfort. Rain down Your Spirit. Pour out Your strength.

575

God, I thank You for not being a distant, unknowable God. I'm so glad that
I can talk to You whenever I want. Here's what's on my heart right now. . . .

576

God, I've been given the responsibility of teaching others about You.
I come to You with empty hands and an open heart. Fill me
with what I need to accomplish Your purposes. Amen.

577

Lord, You know the cause of these tears in my eyes. You know the
sorrows I am carrying. You wept when You saw Your people
hurting. It helps me to know that You share my pain.

578

God, I look up into the night sky and I think about the promise You
made to Abraham. I wonder what promise You have for me. I wonder
where my descendants will go and how many of them there will be. I wonder. . . .

579

Great Provider, You have always been ready to supply all my needs.
I'm facing a financial struggle right now, and I don't know how
to get out of it. Help me place my finances in Your hands.

580

Lord, I need the bravery of Esther today. I need to speak out against injustice, and I'm just not sure how my words will be received. Would You put the best words in my mouth? Would You help me get the attention of the right people?

581

God, help me dwell in patience instead of pointlessness. Help me do what I *can* instead of wishing to live someone else's life. I know every day is a treasure. I know the way I live my life does not reflect that. I want to change.

582

God, sometimes people try to find You in the church, and they can't. There's so much division, so much fighting, so many people communicating conflicting messages. Why can't we all just worship You together?

583

Lord, this whole week has been filled with Mondays. Can I start over? If You could just erase all my mistakes too, that would be great! But I know I must face my own poor decisions. I'm just glad I don't have to do it by myself.

584

Lord, some people think following You will bring them nothing but happiness and success. But I know that following You can be hard—really hard. You told the rich young ruler to sell everything he had in order to follow You. What challenge do You have for me?

585

God, I don't want to ask You this. Honestly, I'm afraid of what Your answer might be. But I'm going to ask You anyway. Lord, whom do You need me to speak to today? Who needs to hear the good news of Your Son and my Savior?

586

Lord God, I wish I had the wisdom of Solomon. But even that wise king made bad decisions when he stopped listening to You. Help me to put You first in my life, in my thoughts, and in my heart.

587

Great Physician, I need Your healing power. I'm sick, and I don't have time to be sick. Please help my body fight off this illness. Please let the medicine work—fast!

588

Open my eyes, Lord. Let me see what You see. Let me hear what You hear. Let me look at strangers and see friends; let me listen to angry voices and hear the longings of lonely hearts. Open my eyes, open my ears, open my mind.

589

God, You don't turn away from those who are suffering. Help me to be like You. Help me to hold the hands of those who are carrying heavy burdens. Help me to share their loads. Help me to offer real help and not empty promises.

590

God, I hold out my empty hands to You and offer all I have, all I am, all I know, all I want, all I can, and all I can't. Take me and use me for Your kingdom. Shape me into a more useful instrument for Your purposes.

591

God, I've been cleaning out my house today, and it struck me that what I need to do is clean out this body that houses my soul. I need You to refine me— to filter out all the impurities. Clean my heart, Lord, and renew my spirit.

592

Jesus, I can't imagine what it must have been like to walk with You as You spoke and taught and healed and ministered to others. I'm so glad I have Your words to learn from. Thank You for making those available to everyone who wants to follow You.

593

God, King David quite rightly acknowledged that "our days on earth are like a shadow, without hope" (1 Chronicles 29:15). But David placed his hope in You, and You placed David in the line of Your Son. And Your Son became the hope of all nations. Thank You, Lord!

594

God, I have nothing to give that doesn't come from You. All I have and all I am was brought to me by Your hand. Help me not to hold so tightly to things of this earth but to be ready to give them all back to You.

595

God, how many times have I turned away from You? How many times have I forgotten to read Your Word? How many times have I been too busy to pray? Yet every time I come back, You accept me and listen to me. Thank You, Lord, for Your mercy.

596

Sleep is running away from me tonight, Lord. My heart is discontented and my mind is troubled. Relationships that used to seem easy are a struggle. Lord, can You show me how to mend them? Can You teach me about Your peace?

597

I was reading Your story today, and I realized that I have not humbled myself, I have not been seeking Your face, and I have not turned from my wickedness. I'm praying to You now to say I will do those things, Lord. Then please, forgive me.

598

God, so many times I let things get in the way of my worship of You. I start to worship money or power or fame or popularity, and before long I can see how weak and powerless those things are. They are nothing like You, Lord. Nothing like You.

599

God, I've been running from You. I know that's ridiculous. I know that I can never hide from You, Lord. But I feel so ashamed, and I'm so angry with myself. I don't want You to see me. And yet, You come looking for me. You come, loving me.

600

Job said, "Even now my witness is in heaven; my advocate is on high. . . . He pleads with God as one pleads for a friend" (Job 16:19, 21). I can't believe that You, Jesus, King of kings and Lord of lords, love me as a friend! Thank You!

601

Lord, are You there? I don't think You have answered me. At least, I don't recognize anything as an answer. Am I just missing it? Lord, I don't understand. How can I know Your will? Look in Your Word? All right, I will.

602

Lord, so many people seem swayed by material things. I find myself getting caught up in this too. I see things I want, and I think I need to have them. God, help me use my resources to extend Your holy kingdom, instead of filling up my house.

603

God, lately I have felt that I am holding too tightly to earthly things. Help me look up. Help me keep focused on You. Help me let go.

604

Lord, Your Word tells me that You hear the "prayer of the righteous" (Proverbs 15:29). But I find it hard to see myself as righteous, though I know Your sacrifice has redeemed my life. Help me to claim my place at Your feet.

605

God, I saw a new baby today. Such a beautiful, peaceful face! So full of life and newness and the promise of good to come. Lord, I want to have a newborn heart. Please grant me fresh eyes, keen ears, and an obedient mind.

606

God, can You hear the desire that is whispering in my soul? I don't even have the words to shape it. I can't put it into a question. I don't have the key to my own heart. Please unlock me, Lord.

607

Lord, I am so ashamed. And yet You welcome me. You reach out Your arms, surrounding me. Somehow You take the hurt I have done and reveal it to me in a way that humbles me and restores me all at once. How do You do that?

608

Lord, I don't want to be the one who is always yelling and losing my temper. Help me be a peacemaker instead. Help me be an example to my whole family. Help me be the first one to say I'm sorry. Let peace begin with me this week.

609

Father, raising obedient, loving children requires me to show gentleness and patience, not threats or harshness. I pray that You will teach me how to soften each correction with the same love I receive from You.

610

Lord, You have shown me how to forgive. Your forgiveness is perfect and comes so freely. Give me the strength to forgive others as You forgive my own trespasses. Help me overlook offenses. Help me cover everything with love.

611

Remember me, Lord. "Do not remember the sins of my youth and my rebellious ways; according to your love remember me, for you, LORD, are good" (Psalm 25:7). And help me remember who You created me to be.

612

Thank You for dealing with my sins so thoroughly, Lord—for granting me a new start every day and proclaiming that I am worth saving. Help me to believe that and to live like I know it.

613

Father, so many people long to be a parent. And I know that longing. Please, Lord, I want Your will to be done in my life. If this is not the path You have chosen for me, I trust in You. I know You have a purpose for me.

....

....

....

....

....

....

614

Father God, it seems my cynical attitude is keeping me from performing acts of hospitality. Please give me the faith and strength to do what needs to be done, not because I want a reward but because it is an honor to do Your work.

615

Lord, You welcomed me into Your family with love and acceptance. Help me be as kind to others as You have been to me. Help me welcome those whom others may reject. Help me offer hospitality to everyone.

616

Father, give me the courage I need to control my fears. I know that You love me and watch over those I love far better than I can. Help me to put my worries about them in Your hands. Strengthen my heart.

617

Lord, many people are traveling today, and the roads are so busy. Please help all the drivers to think clearly and pay attention. Help people to be considerate of one another. And grant us all patience—especially me!

618

"How abundant are the good things that you have stored up for those who fear you, that you bestow in the sight of all, on those who take refuge in you" (Psalm 31:19). God, Your generosity knows no bounds! Thank You!

619

Lord, my anxiety threatens to strangle all the good You have put in my life. Remind me that I am not the one in control. You are the absolute best person to be holding the reins! I can trust You. I can open my hands and relax my hold.

....

....

....

....

....

....

620

Sometimes the words just fall out of my mouth before I even realize I thought them. Help me control my tongue, Lord. I don't want to hurt anyone with harsh judgments or rude replies. Help my words bring glory to You.

621

Father, thank You for making me new! I'm so glad to be able to start again. I can't believe this opportunity I have! I feel like the whole world has been remade, just for me. Thank You, Lord!

622

Lord, I have a friend who is having a hard time. Her troubles keep multiplying. It's not her fault, Lord—it's just life. But she feels like she is drowning. I know I need to lift her up, but I don't know how. Please show me.

623

Please protect my children, Lord. I've tried to instill godly values. I've tried to give them good examples to follow. But I can't be with them all the time. Lord, please keep them from being corrupted and led away from Your truth. Amen.

624

I am grateful for structure, Lord. I am thankful that You have given me clear guidance for what is best for my life. All I have to do is look in Your Word, and I can find answers to my questions. Help me to teach this wisdom to others.

625

Lord, today I am celebrating a life well lived. Please be with the people who are celebrating with me, Lord. There will be a lot of heavy hearts today, because we will all miss this beloved soul. Please remind us all of the hope of heaven.

626

"Send me your light and your faithful care, let them lead me; let them bring me to your holy mountain, to the place where you dwell" (Psalm 43:3). Lord, remind me that You are with me, wherever I go.

627

I don't want to be a waste, Lord. I want to grow to be healthy and strong— like a thick branch of Your vine, bearing good, juicy, life-giving fruit. May the work of my hands benefit others. May my spirit show Your grace.

628

Lord, You are the potter, and I am the clay. Sometimes I wonder how You could make anything beautiful or useful out of me. I feel like I'm a broken pot! But I want to be shaped into a vessel that can be filled up with You.

629

Father, I welcome Your help. You know what I need, and I trust Your provision, knowing You always act in my best interests and want me to have an abundant life. Let me be patient as I wait on You.

630

Lord, so many people on this earth break their promises. It's hard to keep trusting. But You never break a promise. You always keep Your word. Help me to remember what You have promised for me. Help me to keep trusting You.

631

Lord, I am struggling with envy. I saw someone rejoicing today over a victory that I have wanted for a long time. Help me to rejoice when others rejoice—without any hint of bitterness. Help me to be truly happy for them. Help me to depend on You more.

632

Father God, Your grace is sufficient. You are enough for me. I don't have to go searching for anyone else. I don't have to find my strength in anything else. Your power is made perfect in my weakness. Thank You for holding me!

633

God, You never tire of listening to the prayers of Your children. And yet I am exhausted after just one day of hearing others' needs and wants and complaints. Help me persevere. Fill me up with Your strength.

634

"Lord, you have been our dwelling place throughout all generations. Before the mountains were born or you brought forth the whole world, from everlasting to everlasting you are God" (Psalm 90:1–2). And I am forever Yours, Lord!

635

God, I want to know what it means to be truly faithful. I have had some poor examples of faithfulness in my life. But show me, please, what a life of faith looks like. Show me how loyalty and honesty can be lived out. And forgive me when I fail.

....

....

....

....

....

....

636

Lord, when I read the stories of generations long past, I am reminded that You have been working on Your Word—Your love letter to us—for centuries. Thank You for sticking with us, even when we ignore You. Help me not to miss what You have for me in this time.

637

Father, You know how important it is to me to be able to hold my head high. You know how my pride motivates me but also how it can control me. Father, let my boasting be only in You. Crush my prideful heart and make me humble.

638

Lord, I'm grateful that I have the opportunity to teach others the truths that are found in Your Word. I'm trusting that You will increase their spiritual understanding. And I hope You will keep me from confusing them!

639

A dense, chilly fog has settled on the land. And Lord, I can't help thinking about all the times I've let stress sit like a fog on my shoulders, blinding me from seeing the clear, straight rays of Your light. Open my eyes wide, Lord.

640

Father, I thank You for answers to prayer. It is wonderful to know I have a God who delights in hearing and answering my prayers. I am glad to be able to give thanks. Let my tongue never tire of speaking gratitude for You.

641

God, where others speak words of anger and hatred, let me spread Your words of caring and love. Where others sow seeds of discord and strife, let me plant Your peace. Where others seek to steal joy, let me throw a party celebrating life in You!

642

God, the devil does seem to be in the details. He's there in the petty, nagging complaints that arise in my mind every day. He's there in the repeated mistakes. He's there in the sighs and eye rolls. Help me not to let him take hold of my heart!

643

Who else is worthy of praise? Who else is worthy of my worship? Has anyone else set the stars in the sky? Has anyone else set my feet on dry land? Has anyone else defeated death and prepared a place for us in glory? Only You, Lord! Only You!

644

"May God be gracious to us and bless us and make his face shine on us— so that your ways may be known on earth, your salvation among all nations" (Psalm 67:1–2). I pray the glory always and only goes to You, Lord!

645

Lord, as my children grow, help me to treat them like young trees, planting them firmly in Your Word. Then, as I see them getting stronger every day, I pray that they will trust You and be blessed.

646

Lord, You never get tired. You don't ever fail. I am amazed by Your omnipotence. I am awestruck by Your ever-present might. I know I can trust in You. Thank You for showing me Your strength!

647

Almighty God, kids are looking up to role models and superheroes today that are full of flaws. But not You, Lord; You are perfect. Your strength is everlasting. Your justice is sure. Your truth is solid. Please help each new generation to want to follow You.

648

Father, I must be the dumbest sheep in Your flock sometimes. I just keep straying away from You. I keep running off and chasing other things. Thank You for always coming to find me and for bringing me back into Your loving care. You are a Good Shepherd indeed.

649

Lord, I'd like to broadcast Your good news to the nations. Help me tell the story of Your love for us. Let my life be a song of glory to You. Let my feet carry Your message to every person I meet.

650

Father, I feel like I'm being pulled by an invisible force. The temptation is so strong and yet so subtle—sometimes I don't even notice how it has taken hold of my thoughts. Protect my mind, Lord. In the name of Jesus Christ, shut down Satan's lies!

651

Your yoke is easy? Your burden is light? Well, that sounds good to me, Jesus! I'm tired of carrying this heavy load. I'm just plain worn out. I want that rest for my soul, Lord. Here I am.

652

Lord, I know many parents who don't try to see things through their children's eyes. They have no sympathy for the trials their children are facing. But You, our heavenly Father, are not like that. I don't want to be blind to what others are facing either, Lord. Help me to be like You.

653

Sometimes I want to shout at You, Lord. I get so frustrated and so fed up with the suffering of innocent people. I hurt for those who are too weak to protect themselves. I call out to You, Lord. And You show me that You are hurting for them too.

654

Lord, peace is a core of calm, deep inside. No matter what happens to upset us on the surface, You are in our innermost being, bringing peace and comfort. Thank You that we can always trust You.

655

Father, help me be diligent in understanding You and Your precepts. Please give me a continuous desire to know You better. Help my mind never stop wanting to be filled with Your wisdom. Teach me now.

656

True love is kind, not prideful or self-seeking. Lord, fill me with compassion for others so I might be a godly example of love and understanding. I want to show people Your heart, Jesus.

657

Father, help me to cultivate self-control. Don't let me give in to temptation, God! I know I can resist temptation, because You did it, Jesus. Only when I back away from sin can I see the way to follow You. Let me see that path clearly, Lord.

658

Lord, my faith seems weak—not the type of faith that might win any medals. But in You I have the assurance of victory. I've read Your story, and in the end You will reign victorious. I praise You, Lord. I can't wait to see what happens next.

659

"Many, LORD my God, are the wonders you have done, the things you planned for us. None can compare with you; were I to speak and tell of your deeds, they would be too many to declare" (Psalm 40:5). Lord, thank You for _____.

660

Heavenly Father, I can't even begin to count all the good gifts You have given to me! I want to praise You every day! Let me start right now.

661

Lord, You have placed me in the position of instructing others. Let me be a path for Your wisdom to travel to my students. Help me to be firm and forgiving, tender and truthful. Guide me in how to demonstrate love for You and Your laws.

662

Father, remind me that Your standard for relationships is based on respect and love. Let me not forget to be grateful for those who are willing to put up with me, Lord. And when offensive or insulting words leap to my lips, help me to shut my mouth!

663

Father, You are the firm foundation under my feet. I cannot sink as long as I stand on You. The waves may swirl around me; the wind may try to move me. But when I stand on Your solid ground, I will not lose my footing.

664

God, I find it hard not to want You to strike my enemies down, as You did for the Israelites so many thousands of years ago. But I know I must fight my battles in a different way. I must strike them with Your love. Help me to do just that.

665

Father, my trials really do seem light and momentary when I compare them to those of other people. But I remember other times when things went wrong so fast. I cried out to You, and You sent help. Thank You for caring about all my struggles—big or small.

666

God, this particular time in my life doesn't seem to be all that glorious.
I know hard times come to everyone, but I just need to be reminded
of where I'm headed today, Lord. Can You remind me of my hope?

667

Lord, please increase my inner strength. Remind me that although
I seem powerless, Your power knows no limits. You will provide
whatever strength I need to see me through my current crisis.

668

Lord, what You have done for Your people throughout thousands of years
of history just amazes me. Your constant love is so clear to see. On days
when my faith is weak, let me remember Your strength through the ages.

669

God, Your Word tells me that You "bless the righteous; you surround them with your
favor as with a shield" (Psalm 5:12). I need that shield now, Lord. I'm trying to
live by Your laws, but I can feel Satan's arrows coming at me. Help me, Lord!

670

Lord, You promise me wonderful rewards when I am charitable. But I
cannot answer every request made of me, so I count on You to guide
me in knowing where I should invest my efforts to bring You glory.

671
Father, a tiny gift has come into the world. Thank You for Your rich blessings. Thank You for perfectly formed fingers and toes. Thank You for eyes that blink and a wrinkly little nose. Thank You for this precious, priceless present.

672
Lord, so many people quietly work at saving lives every day—nurses, doctors, firefighters, police officers, ambulance drivers, and so many more. Bless the work of their hands. Give them nerves of steel and unending patience, Lord.

673
Lord, I give all my cares to You and try to walk away, but so often I fail. I begin to fear and doubt. I start clawing for control. Forgive me, Lord. Help me to trust You completely. Help me to do what I tell others to do.

674
Lord, Isaiah talks about those who "gladly do right" (Isaiah 64:5). Well, God, I try to do right, but I'm afraid I don't always do it so gladly. Sometimes it's like pulling my own teeth! Help me to have a better attitude in obedience.

675
Lord, help me to remember that there is nothing ahead that I need to fear. Because of You and Your sacrifice, I can claim a victory over sin—every single day. Thank You for making us more than conquerors through You.

676
Lord, this language I speak is so inadequate to tell You what I want to say. I can't begin to find the words to thank You for the successes I have had in my life or to offer my apologies for the messes I've made. But I'll keep trying.

677

Lord, You say there is no condemnation for Your believers, and I trust You. But I have a hard time getting rid of guilt I feel. I keep reliving my sins, wishing I could make them right. Remind me that I don't have to fear punishment. Remind me that I am free.

678

Lord, there are many times when I need You and Your Word to guide me. Lead me to the verses I need to hear the most today. Show me the best examples to follow in my life. Steer me to godly mentors.

679

God, I definitely believe in Your commands. I've seen what happens when people obey You. And I've seen the destruction that can occur when people don't. Teach me knowledge, and grant me good judgment, Lord.

680

I'm ashamed to admit that I often—quite often—speak before I think. The words that come out of my mouth are anything but wise. Help the kids You've entrusted to me to learn from my mistakes and be wise enough to think first then speak.

681

God, when I hear sermons, I have questions. Help me to find good counsel, Lord. Help me to hear Your Word and understand clearly what You mean. I don't want to be confused about what You want from me.

682

In Your Word, Lord, I see Christians being advised not to give up meeting together but to keep encouraging one another. Some days I don't feel like going to church. Help me remember that I need to be with others— to worship You and support the family of God.

....

....

....

....

....

683

Lord, I feel like my family is under attack right now. I know that with
You on our side, we have nothing to fear. Nothing can take us away
from You. Help me to live that out as I live with them.

684

"Teach me, and I will be quiet; show me where I have been wrong" (Job 6:24).
Lord, I echo Job's prayer. I am frightened to have You examine me, and yet
I also long for Your guidance. What I want most is to be closer to You.

685

Lord, guard my tongue as I talk to others and tell them about You.
Season my speech with grace—let me encourage and remind,
educate and reassure. Let me always tell the truth about You.

686

Father, You've given us the best teacher. The Holy Spirit can help me read and
understand Your Word. I want to spend more time searching Your scriptures,
Lord. I want to set aside time that I can spend completely with You.

687

Lord, I need to relax. I need to breathe. In the middle of my day, in the middle of my
week, I feel choked by responsibilities and stress. This feeling kills my productivity,
Lord. Get me over this obstacle, please. Remind me of Your presence.

688

Father, Your grace is so perfect! Your power so overwhelming! Your wisdom
so clear! I am not worthy of Your friendship. Yet You have promised to never
leave me. Help me remember You are with me today as I _____.

689

Lord, I am bored! My hands are idle and my mind is roaming.
Protect me from the temptations that entice me. Give me good work to do.

690

Father God, though Your strength is limitless, it's tempered with wisdom
and gentleness. You are both my strong tower and my tender, loving Father.
Help me to find that proper balance of gentle strength in my own life.

691

I am nothing without You, Lord. When I lose sight of You, I start becoming
filled with fear. Help me to open my eyes. Help me not to let this world cloud
my vision. Help me to hold on to Your hand when I'm walking in the dark.

692

Lord, You are the voice of truth. I need Your help. I'm having trouble knowing
when to speak—when to point out the wrongs people are doing—and when
to be quiet. I don't want to be judgmental. Help me know what to say.

693

Lord, with all the ways that communication happens in our world today,
I feel like it works best face-to-face. Help me to remember
the importance of being with people in person.

694

God, You are a righteous and perfect judge. I have a tendency to jump to conclusions
before I have all the answers. Help me to wait. Help me to listen to others.
Help me to ask good questions. And then, help me to make wise decisions.

695

Lord, You are the one who measures the oceans. You are the one who shapes the land. You are the one who set the stars in the sky and started the planets turning. I praise You for the magnificence of Your creation.

696

God, sometimes we humans balk at being told what to do. We look at laws with suspicion. It is our natural tendency to rebel. I'm asking You today to help me fight against my human nature. Help me to embrace the Holy Spirit living in me.

697

Lord, I want to be sure of what I hope for. I want to be certain about things that I cannot see. I want to live and walk and speak in the confidence that You are not only real, but You love me.

698

Lord, sometimes the law is seen as dry and impersonal. But I delight in Your commands because I know You gave them with me in mind. "Open my eyes that I may see wonderful things in your law" (Psalm 119:18).

699

God, Your angels are a mystery to me. But I know I have felt You guarding and protecting me at several points in my life. I need Your protection today, please.

700

Heavenly Father, this world doesn't look like any kind of heaven! Instead it is full of danger and darkness and disasters! But if I never get out in it, I can't tell others about You. Help me bring the light of Your heaven to others here in the darkness.

701

Father, You've told us who our enemy is. We are not fighting with men and women. We are not fighting with the government. We are not even fighting against ourselves. But we are fighting powers we cannot see. Give me a courageous heart so I can fight for You.

702

Lord Jesus, I know that without You, without the sacrifice You made for me on that cross, I would have no hope. The payment for sin is death, and I have sinned plenty! I thank You today and always for Your sweet saving grace.

703

"Into your hands I commit my spirit; deliver me, Lord, my faithful God" (Psalm 31:5). You are my safe place, Lord. You are my refuge. You are my fortress. Let me rest and be restored in You.

704

God, my God, how can I ever praise You enough? How can I ever express my full thanks for all You've done for me?

....

....

....

....

....

....

....

....

....

705

Father, my heart is breaking. I need to know that You are near and that You care. Gently remind me that You have the power to heal every hurt and to help me make it through what I'm facing right now.

706

Lord, when someone I love is hurt, I want to get revenge. I want to hurt the offender. But I know that is not Your way. Help me to take a step back and try to see the situation through Your eyes.

707

Lord, when I feel anger bubbling up, remind me to take a deep breath, zip my lips, walk away. Help me to take the time to find the right words to express my feelings.

708

Lord, my life is full of distractions, and I have too little time to absorb every sermon the way I should. But You promise You will come into my heart and live there if I welcome You. Come into my heart, Lord Jesus.

709

I repeat the prayer of Moses today, Lord: "If you are pleased with me, teach me your ways so I may know you and continue to find favor with you. Remember that this nation is your people" (Exodus 33:13).

710

Father, I try to give You everything I can, but I feel like
it's not enough. Take my offering and use it to do Your will,
Lord. Help me to give joyously, generously, and humbly.

711

Lord, I trust You with my life on earth, and I trust You to give
me eternal life. And yet so many times I doubt I'm going to
make it to the next day! Help me, Lord, to trust You more.

712

Lord, sometimes I feel so afraid. Please help me remember where my strength
and salvation come from. Help me say with confidence, "Whom shall I fear?"

713

God, there wasn't ever a word that came from Your mouth that wasn't well
placed and well timed and well used. I want to be like You! I know my
speech will never be perfect, but I have a lot of room for improvement!

714

Thank You for sleep, Lord—for blessed rest. Thank You for a time to
relax and unwind. Thank You for the nights when You still my troubled
soul so I can close my eyes and be at peace—even if it's just for a few hours.

715

Father, pursuing happiness can lead me to a dead-end road at times.
Help me to realize, and remember, that You are the source of my joy.
Let me find happiness in the moments when I feel closest to You.

716

Lord, my heart feels bound up by tight cords of negative emotions—
fear, disappointment, bitterness, guilt, resentment, suspicion,
and jealousy. Cut through these cords, God. Free my heart.

717

God, I'm having so much trouble concentrating. As soon as I begin to speak
to You, something or someone distracts me. Help me to shut everything
else out—just for a few minutes, Lord. I just want to think about You.

718

"Since you are my rock and my fortress, for the sake of your name lead and
guide me. Keep me free from the trap that is set for me, for you are my refuge"
(Psalm 31:3–4). God, I'm trusting You to protect me. I know You will.

719

Wow, Lord. That was definitely a wrong turn. I can't believe I couldn't see
that coming. Protect me from making stupid mistakes, God. Help me to
think more clearly. I want to gain wisdom and understanding, Lord.

720

Direct my steps, God. Only You know where I need to be—and when
I need to be ready to join in Your work. Right or left, I ask You to turn me.
I'm not always good at following directions, Lord. Just give me a shove!

721

Father, I admit that every now and then I just lose it. I lash out. I mope.
I throw a pity party. I even get mad at You. Thank You for Your love and
patience in these times. Thank You for always redirecting my course.

722

When Your purpose is revealed to me, Father, help me to accept
my responsibility and do Your will. I know I'm stubborn,
Lord, and sometimes I resist You. Don't give up on me!

723

Father, it often seems that I stand no chance against the evil plots
of people who don't know You. But I know Your power can overcome
any plans. Renew my faith in Your righteous justice, Lord.

724

I often feel like Your promises must be for someone else, Lord. I can't
imagine that You are talking to me. I don't feel faithful enough. I don't
feel like I deserve Your attention. Show me the error of this thinking.

725

Examine me. Search me. Dig out the deception, uncover my lies,
reveal all the truth. Let me face all the evil I have swallowed so
I can get rid of it, Lord. Let me be cleaned and renewed by You.

726

Thank You, Lord, for what I do have. Help me be wise with how I use all my
resources—my time and my money and the talents You have given me. I know
that what seems like little to me could go a long way in Your kingdom.

727

Lord, I can find happiness in a lot of places. But it's hard
for me to find joy in obedience sometimes. Please help
me find the freedom that comes with obedience to You.

728

Lord, there have been times when I so clearly heard Your voice and felt You
nudging me in a certain direction. That was amazing. I love it when I
am in tune with Your will. Help me get tuned in to You right now.

729

Lord, I long to feel Your touch, hear Your voice, and see Your face. Whatever
comes to me this day, I know You will be with me, as You are now—
within me, above me, beside me. Thank You for strengthening my heart.

....

....

....

....

....

....

....

....

730

My Shepherd, my Lord, my Savior, lead me beside the still waters. Lie with me in the green pastures. Restore my soul. With You by my side, I can go anywhere without fear. Thank You for Your goodness and Your mercy—this minute, this hour, and this day.

731

You defend me, You love me, You lead me. How great is that! How great are You! This morning, in Your presence, I rejoice. I direct my prayers to You, knowing that You will hear me.

732

Lord, You are my strength and my shield. You give me courage to meet the challenges of the day. You build me up, raise me to the heights, and lead me to places I would never have dreamed were possible. With You in my life, I can do anything.

733

Lord, when I am in the wilderness, You tell me not to fear. I thirst for Your presence and am rewarded with Your peace. You open my eyes and direct me to the living water. Lord, there is no one who loves me as You do.

734

As I spend time with You, Lord, my strength is renewed. I soar like the eagles. I feel as though I could run forever and never grow weary. Be with me here and now, today and forever.

735

Lord, my pilot and guide, give me direction this day. You teach me what is best for me and direct me in the way I should go. When I pay attention to Your commands, You give me peace like a river. Help me obey You in all I say and do.

736

God, sometimes life is so messy. Nothing has been going right. All I want
to do is throw up my hands in frustration. Yet You are not a God of
disorder but a God of peace. Help me rest in Your presence, Lord.

737

Lord, I seem to be always on the run. Calm my heart and my soul.
Make my thoughts clear. I come seeking Your peace, resting in
Your arms. Speak to me in this small bit of silence I have found.

738

Provider God, I remember the times You've taken care of me, suffered with me,
and led me through the darkness. I feed on these memories. I feed on Your
faithfulness. Remain with me now, giving me courage and strength as I trust in You.

739

It is my faith in You, Jesus, that keeps me sane and gives me peace. I am
eternally grateful for that peace, and I thank You. My faith in You justifies
me and gives me the grace I need to forgive others. Help me do that today.

740

God, I am filled with a sinking-like-Peter feeling right now. Buoy my faith,
Lord, so I can stand firm. As I meditate on how You control the wind
and the waves, fill me with Your power, courage, and strength.

741

Each time I come to You, Lord, You open the eyes of my heart and fill me
with Your awesome resurrection power. As I seek Your face, I am filled with
endless hope. I revel in Your glorious riches. I await Your words, dear Lord!

742

What incredible joy fills my soul! I love You, Lord, and I am filled with
Your love for me. Words cannot express the glorious joy I feel at this moment,
basking in Your light, warmed by Your presence. Never leave me, Lord!

743

Lord, I read in Your Word about the miracles You have performed,
and I find myself wondering if You can make miracles happen
in my life today. I place my heart's desire before You.

744

Holy Spirit, it all comes down to faith in God. Fill my heart with assurance,
with confidence, and with the promise from Jesus that everything is possible
for those who believe. Clear my mind, soul, and spirit of any lingering doubts.

745

Lord, from the beginning of time, You have been the one true God.
You are the Ancient of Days. I humbly come before You, earnestly seeking
Your face. I stagger at the weight of Your might and power. Hear my prayer.

....

....

....

....

....

....

....

....

....

746

"Rise and go; your faith has made you well" (Luke 17:19).
Thank You, Jesus, for Your words. May I rise from this place
of prayer full of faith that heals my mind, body, and spirit.

747

Lord, I want to do what You have created me to do. I come seeking Your
direction for my life. I have my own ideas of how You want me to serve You,
but I need Your wisdom. When and where and how shall I go? Lead me, Lord.

748

God, Your creation is truly awesome. Everywhere I look, I see Your
handiwork. You have made it all. You have made me. Continue
to mold me and shape me into the person You want me to be.

749

I cannot see what the future holds, but I know You can, Lord. You hold
the future in Your hands. Open my ears to Your voice and my eyes to Your
creative vision for my life. Help me to see where You want me to go next.

750

Oh God, before I was even conceived, You loved me. You have set me apart
for a special purpose, for a way to achieve Your ends. I am nothing without You,
yet You ask me to be a part of the grand plan. Here I am, Lord! Use me!

751

I know what You want me to do, Lord. I hear Your voice telling me
how You want me to serve. Help me to put aside my doubts,
misgivings, and fears. I want to go where You command.

....

....

....

....

....

....

752

Sometimes, Lord, when I seek advice, I look for counsel from people who don't know much about me. Sometimes I just look for people who will agree with me. God, push me to ask for help from the people who know my history. Let me seek real, honest conversations.

753

With all my personality quirks, You've made me the way I am for a reason. You are the author and finisher of my faith. For now and always, You are here to help me. Thank You for leading me into the light of Your Word.

754

Lord, I am Your child, and that means I am a child of peace. When someone strikes me on the left, I need to turn my head, instead of striking back. I can only do this through Your power, Lord. Help me to stay close to You.

755

Lord, sometimes people get called to do the small things. I hear You calling me to do some small tasks—things that don't come with glory or fame or even pats on the back. Help me persist in this work. Humble me, Lord, to do Your will.

756

No matter what I face today, Lord, You are going before me. You will lead me through the desert, sustaining me with Your living water. When I am tired, You will carry me. Help me to persevere in that hope!

757

Nothing will cause me dismay, nothing will discourage me with You by my side, oh Lord of my life. Help me seek Your advice first. Help me hear Your Word first. Before I move, before I speak, before I act—let me seek You.

758

Lord, don't let me stumble, please. Eliminate the obstacles of worry and fear that line the path before me. Give me hope and courage to face my future. Give me a clear mind to make the right decisions. Let me walk with You.

759

Dear God, I feel plagued by the what-ifs that tumble through my mind and pierce my confident spirit. Help me trust in Your wisdom and power to guide me so that I may be ready for any changes that come.

760

Through Your Word, I know that "the eyes of the LORD range throughout the earth to strengthen those whose hearts are fully committed to him" (2 Chronicles 16:9). It comforts me to know You are looking out for me, Lord. I commit myself to You.

761

God, all my plans are in ruins. The things I have desired are out of my reach. Wipe the tears of frustration and disappointment from my eyes, Lord. Help me to keep my focus on You and not on my momentary troubles.

762

With one glance, You see all the generations that have gone before, that are present now, and that will come in the future. You see it all! Allow me to rest in the knowledge that each and every day You go before me.

763

God, You know these are hard times. You know how much money this household needs to function. Hear my prayer and help me do my part in providing for my family. Help us to keep this roof over our heads.

764

Oh Lord, what a promise You have made to me, that You will supply all I need through Christ (Philippians 4:19)! Let my prayer time be more than utterances of what I desire; let it be a time of fellowship with You, knowing my needs are provided.

765

I watch in hope for You, Lord. I wait expectantly for You to answer the petitions I make to You today. Give me the gift of patience as I wait for Your response. Help me not to run ahead of You but to wait and pray and hope.

766

Lord, sometimes I don't understand why it takes so long for You to answer some of my prayers. At times Your answers are immediate, but on other occasions I need to keep coming before You. Help me grow in the waiting time, Lord.

767

Lord, help me to give back to You, even when it feels like I don't have anything to give. I want to show You how much I love and trust You. I need to let go of my fears and my desire for control. Help me, Lord.

768

God, I'm so thankful for the many practical ways You provide for me and those I love. I see Your wise provision in so many aspects of my life. Here are just a few things I want to thank You for. . . .

769

Lord, because of You, I have all I need. You continually shower blessings on me. Sometimes I don't even see all the ways You are watching over me. Help me to know You more so I can see how You are working in my life.

770

Day by day, Lord, You have met my needs in this land afflicted with greed and intolerance. Right now in Your presence I feel Your life springing up within me. Thank You for Your living water that never fails to refresh and restore.

771

Lord, I humble myself before You, bowing down at Your throne. I still can't believe You even allow me to come to You, King of kings. Your grace amazes me. Your love surprises me. Your compassion moves me. I worship You.

772

God, I know I don't have to worry about those who wish to harm me. I don't have to pay attention to the insults of those who want to tear me down because You, who hold the universe in Your hands, are building me up. And that is enough!

773

God, water erodes mountains and knocks down cities. Yet You can calm the oceans. No one else has that power! What do I have to be afraid of when the tide of my troubles rushes in? You can take care of me.

774

Your instruction keeps me on the right path, and for that I praise You, Lord. Thank You for giving me Your holy Word, to have and to hold. You are the great communicator. I trust in Your Word, for when I'm armed with it, I am not afraid.

775

As I sit here before You, Lord, I want to praise You with my whole heart. I praise You with my lips, my voice, my mouth, my life. Please accept my sincere praise as I humble myself before You.

776

When I am weak, Your strength upholds me. When I am afraid, Your courage sustains me. When I am downcast, Your presence lifts me. You are always there for me. How great, how wonderful, how amazing You are, my God, my friend, my Father!

777
Lord, give me a compassionate heart. Lead me to the concern You would like me to champion for You, whether it's working in a soup kitchen, helping the homeless, or adopting a missionary couple.

778
Dear God, today I lift up world leaders—presidents, premiers, kings, queens, prime ministers, ambassadors, and all rulers. Give them wisdom to rule well, give them courage to fight oppression, and give them minds that seek and love peace.

779
Lord, I've been praying a long time about this situation that doesn't ever seem to change. I'm asking You now, what should I do? Is it time for a different plan? Lead me to people who aren't afraid to speak truth into my life.

780
Lord, sometimes I want to say, "Beam me up, God!" I want to escape this place, with all its troubles and temptations. But I know You have work for me to do here. Let me help the hungry, the oppressed, the imprisoned, the homeless, and the wounded.

781
Dear God, I pray for peace throughout the world. Some say it's impossible—but with You all things are possible! Peace does not yet reign throughout the earth, but it can reign in my heart. Let me start there and spread that peace to others.

782

Lord, I want to work with one mind and spirit together with others in Your church (Philippians 2:2). Help me to value others above myself. Help me to focus on the interests of the body of believers. Help us all to live in unity.

783

God, through the divine power of Your Spirit and Your Word, I pray for my neighborhood. Demolish the stronghold of evil within my community. Touch each heart with Your peace. Help me to be an ambassador for You, right here and right now.

784

Lord, You tell me that I am the light of the world (Matthew 5:14). Help me to shine my light for You. Help me to bring hope to my friends and neighbors. Help me to spread Your message of love for all.

785

Dear Lord, so many people in this world are hurting from cycles of violence, abuse, addiction, and crime. Touch those who suffer. Cover them with Your protection. Give them assurance of Your presence. And guide me to know how to give practical help.

786

Lord, please soften the hardened hearts of those who are cultivating hatred and spreading terror. Exchange their hearts of stone for ones tender with love. Protect the innocent here and abroad. Amplify the message of Your love around the world.

787

Lord, I pray that You would oust the unseen evils from this land.
I pray that Your angels would battle fiercely against the dark forces
corrupting youth. Empower those who minister to, teach, coach,
and lead youth. Give them wisdom and compassion as they reach out.

788

Lord, may Your hand be on missionaries and pastors, guarding them
from the devil's attacks. Protect them in their waking and sleeping hours.
Give them the endurance to do what You have called them to do.

789

Lord, help me not to forget those who are not often in my sight.
Help me to honor the elderly, to care for the chronically ill, and to
support the caregivers. Let me serve them with a humble heart.

790

The world may pass away, but Your love never fails. Those who believe in You
will live with You forever. What a blessed thing! I pray that others around the
world will hear the message so that they too can accept Your gift of eternal life.

791

Lord, clothe me with Your compassion, kindness, humility, gentleness,
and patience (Colossians 3:12). Let those who need help be able
to trust me. Let them see that I am wearing Your love, Lord.

792

Lord, there are many dark forces at work in our schools, on our streets, and in our homes. I pray for Your light to eliminate the evil among us. You have overcome this world, Jesus. Give me the heart to intercede for others and the courage to protect the weak.

793

I want to work for You, Lord, using all my heart, soul, and talent. I want to be Your tool, serving You with passion. Help me to keep my focus on You and not on the gift You've given me.

794

God, I know You've planned good things for me to do. But doing good things doesn't mean doing easy things. Help me not to shy away from the challenges that face me.

795

Everyone has different gifts, Lord—I know that. Help me to figure out how to work with others well so that we can achieve Your purposes. Amen.

796

Lord, I know I am supposed to do my work as if I'm doing it for You, rather than for any boss here on earth. But sometimes it is very difficult to remember that. Help me to focus always on pleasing You first.

797

God, You have given me all that I need to do Your will. Today I
feel strong, bold, and fearless. I am ready, willing, and able
to do all that You call me to do. Where should I start?

798

Give me the passion, Lord, to serve You well. I struggle with maintaining the
kind of enthusiasm I first had when I started serving You. Set my spirit on fire,
Lord! Fill me up with Your presence. Give me eager eyes and ready hands.

799

Remind me, Lord, that my service to You is a way to honor You.
You have done so much for me. Allow me to use my gift to bring greater
glory to Your name so that others will be drawn ever closer to You.

800

Jesus, when You washed the dirty, dusty feet of Your disciples, I think I
know how they must have felt. It's the way I feel every time I think
of all You've done for me—thankful, overwhelmed, shocked,
and stunned. May I follow Your example in serving others.

801

I worship You with my hands, making them dirty as I clean for You. I worship You
with my feet, rubbing blisters on them as I travel to serve my city. I worship You with
my tongue, telling Your good news. Give me strength to keep serving You, Lord.

802

Lord, better than any doctor, You know what is attacking my body right now. I ask You to fill me with Your healing power. Move this sickness away from my house. Grant me the rest and strength I need to recover quickly.

803

Lord, I am aching, but not in my flesh. My heart is hurting for Your children. So many are lost; so many are hopeless. They think they are all alone in this world. Help me to show them the truth—that You are always with them.

804

When I am weak, I am made strong through my dependence on Your power. And if that's the best way for people to see You, Lord, then let me be weak.

805

Lord, I pray for _____, who needs Your healing touch. Like the woman who followed You through the crowds just to touch Your cloak, my friend has so much faith in You, Lord. I have faith too. I know You can deliver relief.

806

Lord, You are the healer of our wounds, the one who restores spirit, soul, and body. Thank You for blessing my life through Your holy touch. Thank You for covering over my wounds with Your love and care.

807

Help me to have the courage of Daniel, Lord. When I face opposition
for my beliefs—when people around me ridicule or belittle my faith—
let me fight back by continuing to serve You faithfully and visibly.

808

God, You heal the brokenhearted and bind up their wounds (Psalm 147:3).
So I come to You with the pieces of my heart today. No one understands, but I
know I can talk to You. Let me sit here with You and tell You what happened. . . .

809

Bless You, Lord! Bless Your holy name! Let everything within me
praise You. Let my soul remember all that You've done for me.

810

I know You know the number of the hairs on my head, Lord. Do You know the
number of my tears too? I imagine that You do. And You care about each one.
Thank You for hearing my prayers and seeing my tears. Thank You for loving me!

811

I opened Your Word today, Lord, looking for some encouragement.
And soon I found the words I needed: "I sought the Lord, and he answered
me; he delivered me from all my fears" (Psalm 34:4). Thank You, Lord!

....

....

....

....

....

....

....

....

....

812

Almighty God, You command Your angels to surround me and protect me.
Help me to feel that protection so that I won't live in fear. Let me step
out boldly into the world, knowing You will guard me and guide me.

813

God, some people are doing some scary things all over the world. And that terror
has crept into my community. But I refuse to be driven by despair and fear.
I will not bow to my own insecurities. Instead, I will put my trust in You.

814

Lord, You have always been my hope—my only constant hope. Sometimes
I'm afraid to step outside or even watch the news. It seems like every
day brings some new terrible story. But I remember that my hope
is in You, not in this world, and that helps.

815

Jesus, You warned us. You told us there would be trouble in this world.
But You also told us that You had overcome the world. So I will
take heart. I will be encouraged. I will live boldly in You.

816

With You as my helper, Lord, what can anyone here on this earth really
do to me? My soul belongs to You. My flesh may fail me, and I may
get hurt in my body. But my heart and my spirit are safe with You.

817

My to-do list keeps growing, Lord. I don't feel like I'm making any real progress. Help me to stay focused on what is important. Help me not to get distracted by small matters. I want to walk in Your will and not mine.

818

Lord, I don't want to be like some people, running around and doing too many things at once. Change my way of thinking to Your way of thinking. I take my list of goals and place it in Your hands. Help me see this list through Your eyes.

819

Lord, I know I need to seek Your kingdom first. But what does that mean? I think it means that I should look first at the things that will make Your kingdom grow— loving You and loving others. Help me to understand this better, Lord.

820

Lord, show me how to love those people I come into contact with through my daily routine. Help me be a person of compassion, even in the slightest interactions. When people see me, I want them to recognize You.

821

God, Jacob wrestled with an angel, and sometimes I feel like I'm trying to wriggle out of the hold You have on me—and I don't even know why! Help me calm my rebellious spirit, Lord. Help me serve and obey You.

....

....

....

....

....

....

....

....

....

822

Lord, we are packing up and moving again. Help me get my family settled as quickly as possible, Lord. Help us to meet new friends soon. And help us to find a church family that will welcome us.

823

A purring kitten. A sleeping puppy. A swaddled newborn. A baby bird, opening its mouth for its dinner. All these images make me feel both comforted and the desire to give comfort. Thank You for the natural instincts You have set in us all, Lord.

824

I had a nightmare last night, Lord. I watched a scary movie and the images stained my mind. Help me to make good choices about what I allow to sink into my brain, Lord. Help me to choose things that can be used for Your glory.

825

God, I feel like Moses—my words come slowly and with hesitation. I am not a strong speaker, Lord. Help me find my voice. Help me to be prepared to tell someone why I have hope in You.

826

God, I am not good about taking care of this body You have given me. I have a hard time with discipline in this area. Help me to know that when I am exercising, I am equipping myself for service in Your kingdom.

827

Lord, my mind is weighed down with depression. Help me to find someone who can guide me to useful treatment. I don't want to lose any more days, Lord. Time is too precious. And I have so much I want to do with You!

828

Lord, I need to let go. It's time to let my children have some independence, and after all these years, that's hard to do. Help me to know deep in my heart that You will protect them. You love them more than I ever could.

829

Healer and Lord, You know our bodies are so fragile and easily injured. I know so many people right now who have bruises and breaks and sprains and wounds. Please mend these hurting bodies. And please give them the comfort only You can bring.

830

Lord, we have so many ways to reach each other these days, but somehow they seem to make us more lonely at times. We are disconnected and distracted. We don't take time for long, heart-to-heart conversations. Slow me down, Lord. Help me make real connections.

831

God, may I strive for excellence in all that I do—not for recognition or a raise or words of praise, but as a gift of gratitude to You. Let me offer You the work of my hands. And let that offering be the best that I can make it.

832

God, people are having a hard time figuring out what is truth and what is not. I need to remember to always look to You first to make these judgments. Help me be consistent in my message. Help me to speak the truth.

833

What does the world need now? The song says "love," and that answer sounds right to me. God, pour out Your love on our world. Let it spread through Your churches and out into the nations.

834

My thoughts swirl around the latest news stories of the day. And as the headlines enter my mind, my anxieties grow. Help me not to be overwhelmed by events that are not important in the grand scheme of things, Lord.

835

I lay myself before You, Your willing servant. May everything I do today leave a good impression of You. Help me to be a blessing to the people I interact with throughout my day.

836

I think of all the good men and women who have had an impact on my life and I'm so thankful for their examples of godly living, Lord. They taught me things without ever opening their mouths. I pray my life has such an impact!

837

I want to rest here at Your feet, Lord. I want to touch Your robe,
hear Your voice. When I do Your work today, everything else will
fall into place. I lean back, waiting to hear You speak.

838

Lord, You have made me both a symbol and a source of blessing to others.
I will be strong, confident in the benefits You bring, able to stretch myself as I
strive to reach others so that they too will have the goodness of Your blessings.

839

God, I pray that You will bless those who have not been kind to me. Help me
not to repay evil with evil but to respond in kindness. Give me the strength
to keep my anger and frustration at bay. Give me love that will let me forgive.

840

I will not worry about what I eat, wear, drink, or earn today.
No, I am content, leaving all my concerns for my well-being in
Your hands, knowing that You will provide. You are first in my life.

841

This way of life, enveloped by Your presence, living God, is the true way. Keep my
feet sure on this path. Take care of me through this day and the days to come.

Lord, give me the courage to pursue the dreams You have for me. I'm not sure where those dreams will take me or what I will do, but I know I will be safe in Your hands.

843

Lord, I want to be a better friend. Help me be trustworthy, devoted, and reliable. Help me put the desires of my friends before my own. Give me the power of encouragement so that I may be at their side.

844

What an example of love You give us, Jesus! You laid down Your life for everyone—even while we were still sinners. Fill me with that kind of self-sacrificing love, Lord. Give me the ability to love those who do not love me.

845

Lord, I have been blessed with good friends. I continue to be amazed at the beautiful hearts You have placed inside Your people. Thank You for surrounding me with wonderful examples of faith-filled lives.

846

Lord, I want to build people up. Words can be so painful, and I've let many hurtful ones pass my lips. I want to stop that now, God. Help me to control what I say. Give me words that are sweet to the soul.

847

Holy Spirit, carry me to a place where I can find my breath,
where I can sit in silence. I need You to lift me up, above all these
problems. I need some time—some time to think about You.

848

Lord, it's time. I need to tell someone about You. Give me the right moment,
the right words. Let me listen well. Please be in our midst, oh Lord, as my friend
considers the most important decision of a lifetime!

849

God, I remember how Peter's friends prayed for him while he was in prison, how they
constantly and consistently interceded for him. Help me to be that kind of prayer
warrior today. Bring the names to my mind that need Your help, Lord.

850

God, so many men and women give up so much to serve our country. Please bless
them. Give them strength and protection. Give them endurance for the long days
and nights. Heal their minds and hearts when they receive wounds that go deep.

851

Lord, so many different people are part of Your church. Make us together
a unified body, strengthened by Your Spirit and bound together
with Your love. Help us grow closer to each other and to You.

852

Lord, open my mind and heart and ears to Your voice today. Still the constant chatter in my head, reminding me of all the tasks that I need to get done. Lead me step-by-step, Lord. I commit my way and my plans to You.

853

I'm in awe of Your creativity. I want to make beautiful things too, Lord. You inspire me. The works of Your hands are more majestic than anything I could create. But if I can capture just a glimpse of You, I will feel successful.

854

Lord, I don't know why I do it, but I do keep a record of wrongs. I keep bringing up old offenses. Help me to put the past behind me. Help me to really forgive. And when I do remember old wounds, help me not to use them against others.

855

Jesus, I am mad at myself. I have been doing wrong and hiding it from everyone. I even imagined I could hide it from You. Please forgive me for not admitting my sins. Help me to do better. I don't want to live this way anymore.

856

Lord, I've crashed into a wall. I'm engaged in a conflict I don't know how to resolve. You are able to mend relationships and bring peace. Please show me how to build a bridge over the gap that separates me from _____.

857

Father, I know that I judge people. I may not say the words or treat people differently in public, but in my own thoughts, in my heart, I know that I put people into categories that I don't like to admit. Lord, help me see everyone as You do.

858

God, search me today. See if there is anything in me that is
cruel or harsh or hurtful. Root out coldness and bitterness
and negativity. Hold me up to Your light. Make me new.

859

I'm celebrating Your victory over death today, Lord. Jesus lives!
I know it's true, and I'm so astounded by that fact. I want to tell everyone.
Help me to spread the good news of Your amazing, death-defeating love.

860

Lord, I've been talking aimlessly again. Please correct my path.
Help me not to engage in thoughtless gossip. I'm carrying stories in
my mind that I should not know. Help me not to spread rumors, Lord.

861

God, it would be so easy to waste this day. It would be so easy to
just do nothing, say nothing, and care about nothing. Help me
not to be lazy. Shove me out the door if You have to, God!

862

Lord, shake up my world. I'm tired of being complacent. I'm tired of seeing stories of
others' pain and just watching and sitting and letting those stories pass me by without
any action on my part. Show me what I can do—even in this moment.

863

Redeemer, I am weighed down and bound up by chains of guilt. Set me free, Lord! Break these chains! Help me not to just know Your salvation in my head but to work it out in my life with fear and trembling in the shattering joy of grace.

864

Lord, it's stunning to think of You humbling Yourself to come to this dirty earth as a helpless babe wrapped in rags and laid down in a feeding trough. Only my God is so huge that He could become so small to save the world. Amazing God!

865

Lord, You are able to change the hearts of kings. You are able to sway even the most stubborn soul. I've got someone in mind, Lord. You know who it is. Break down their locked-up life! Soften this hardened, wounded heart.

866

God, I'm pulling on my socks and getting ready for my day and suddenly I think—this is the day that You have made. For me. You are watching me, Lord. You see me. Where do You want me to go next?

867

God, it has been a long day. So much work. So many hours. And all for what? Sometimes I can't see the purpose. Help me to see the reason I live, Lord. Help me to understand what I'm here for.

....

....

....

....

....

....

....

....

868

Lord, I've heard some hurtful things. Harsh criticism has come to my ears, and all I want to do is run. Help me to pull out the grains of truth, Lord, that are mixed in with the chaff. Help me to see if there is anything I need to change.

869

Lord, I want to be grafted into Your vine and grow with You. I want to be part of the work that is bearing good fruit. I want to see a great harvest of souls! Show me what to do.

870

Tune my heart to sing Your praise, Lord. Let my worship be purely about You and never about my need to show off or be seen as holy. Let me become part of this body, blended in and committed as one to praise Your precious name.

871

Lord, I turn the pages of this book and I think about how You are writing my life. You know my past. You know what I'm doing right now. And You know what's coming next. Help me to trust You as author of my life.

872

God, I can't keep up with the way my world is changing. I don't feel prepared to handle the trials that I know are coming. God, help me not to mess this up!

873

Jesus, I come to Your table today to remember You. I come to sip from the cup and accept Your promise of a new covenant. I come to break the bread and envision how You were broken for me. Lord, I bow in gratitude for Your sacrifice.

874

God, I tried to help a friend and I was rejected. Help me to get over the hurt. Help me to understand why it happened. And help me to repair this friendship. I know I need to say I'm sorry, but I'm not sure what I did. Can You show me?

875

Lord, I come to You today with a painful topic. I want You to help my church family forgive those leaders who have violated the trust of the members. It's a big task, Lord, but I know You can bring us peace.

876

Lord, thank You for _____, who has been an unwavering example of faithfulness to me. I'm so amazed and humbled by the way this person keeps going, no matter what comes. I love it when I can see You so clearly in the hearts of Your people, Lord.

877

Lord, sometimes when I go to church and listen to the sermon, I find there is a critical spirit at work in my heart. Please help me to silence the voice of negativity and listen to the truth of Your Word.

878
God, I'm physically sore today. Muscles I didn't even know I had are crying out in pain with every move I make. But I have to keep moving and fulfill my tasks for today. Help me do my best!

879
Help me to prioritize my to-do list today, Lord. Help me to be able to do the things that I need to do, and help me let go of the rest. I know I can't do it all!

880
God, sometimes I listen to the voices of people who call themselves Christians and I feel embarrassed, even ashamed. And then I wonder if You ever feel that way about me. God, I pray that I can be someone who makes You proud.

881
Oh Lord, I looked up at the star-studded sky tonight and I felt the massiveness of the universe. And I felt my own smallness and vulnerability. Protect me, Lord, from those forces that would seek to destroy me.

882
Lord, I understand eternal. I have some never-ending activities in my life. Every time I think I'm finished, there is another thing to do. I look forward to Your promised heaven, Lord, when I'll be set free from this earthly cycle!

883
God, I breathe and think about how You knew me before I ever took my first breath in this world. I move and know You loved me before the world was set into motion. Thank You for Your forever love!

884

God, I hate it when I hear about people hurt by other Christians. If I can do anything to heal their wounds, Lord, let me do it. If I can in any way be a balm for their disappointed hearts, let me be it.

885

God, I've got a chance to speak for You today. I've got an opportunity to change minds and impact hearts. Take my words, Lord, and make them Yours. Weave them into the message You want people to hear.

886

I am an empty vessel, waiting to be filled with Your Spirit, Lord. Pour Your Spirit into my life. Fill me up to overflowing so I can spread Your joy, peace, and love to a world that needs it so much.

887

Sometimes I think we make a mistake, God. We think the pastors and priests who lead our churches are supposed to be perfect. But they make mistakes too. They are human. Help me to forgive them, God, just as You forgive me.

888

Lord, a blank page sits before me. I need to write someone and say I'm sorry, and I just don't know where to start. Guide me to words, Lord, that will express what's truly on my heart.

....

....

....

....

....

....

....

....

889

God, I've been noticing some things—acts of injustice, hatred, and rebellion. I place these things before You. Help me to know how to fight against these acts with truth, love, and obedience.

890

God, I'm fed up! Someone keeps irritating me on purpose, and I have had enough! I know I'm supposed to turn the other cheek, but what can I do to stop this behavior? Show me the way of wisdom, Lord. I don't want to do anything rash or stupid.

891

Wow, Lord! You have created such a beautiful world! I can't describe the majesty of Your mountains, the magnificence of Your seas, or the mystery of Your universe—but I'm so glad I get to know their Maker!

892

Your mercy, Lord, keeps my feet on solid ground. I don't deserve Your forgiveness, but You keep giving it to me anyway. Every time I stumble, You are there, holding me up. Thank You for Your presence!

893

Jesus, I know You said that if we have faith, we can move mountains, but I don't know about this one that I'm facing just now. It's a mountain of trouble, and it's massive, Lord. Take my little faith and make it grow, please.

....

....

....

....

....

....

....

....

894

When I can't control my anger, I know it gives the devil a chance to control me, Lord. Help me to have a spirit of forgiveness and reconciliation instead of bitterness and retribution. Give me Your powerful, peaceful, anger-melting love!

895

God, it's beautiful to see two become one. I pray for a newlywed couple, Lord. I pray You bless their union and let them grow closer together every day. And when the bumps in their road come along, I pray that You encourage them to hold tight to each other.

896

Love never gives up. Love *never* gives up. God, help me not to quit either.

897

Lord, relationships are hard work! I don't feel like I had enough training before I started this one! Help me to figure things out, Lord. Help me to ask for help. Help me to be a better friend, a better partner, and a better representative of Your love.

898

Rough, weathered hands. Wrinkled smiles in wrinkled faces. Silver hair and cloudy eyes. Lord, help me love the elderly. Show me their stories. Let me honor their lives.

....

....

....

....

....

....

....

....

....

....

899

God, sometimes it seems impossible to keep loving someone—especially when that someone seems to run away from my love. Help me to keep trying, Lord. But help me also not to neglect others in my life in the process. I need to know the right balance, Lord.

900

Lord, as I lay my head down on my pillow tonight, I pray for sleep to come easily. I ask You to bring me peaceful sleep that allows my body to be restored and my mind to be refreshed. Watch over me all through the night.

901

Lord, there is tension in my house, and I hate it. I want to fix it. I've said I'm sorry, but it doesn't seem to be enough. Help me to know what else I should do, Lord! And help me to forgive and love again.

902

Lord, I'm feeling sad today about days gone by. Help me not to get stuck in this sorrowful spirit, Lord. Show me the goodness and glory in my present world. Give me a glimpse of future adventures. Renew my desire to embrace life!

903

Lord, it's time to say goodbye, but I'm having trouble. I just can't let go. I don't want to forget. I don't want to move on. Lord, sit with me in my grief. Be my comfort and my peace. And help me have the strength to get through this.

904

Lord, I'm waiting for You to speak. I'm waiting on Your words of wisdom.
Open my eyes, my heart, and my spirit to understanding Your will.
Guide my words to others today. Let me build them up, Lord.

905

God, people are hurting each other for ridiculous reasons. I don't understand
the willingness to do evil at the slightest provocation. God, shock us with
Your justice. Shine Your brilliant light of righteousness in our faces,
Lord, until we all stop and pay attention.

906

God, I am angry. I read about another child hurt today, and I am burning with
rage at those who inflicted such pain on this innocent one. God, take my anger and
turn it into something holy. Take it and use it to fuel even just one helpful act.

907

God, the birds are singing, praising Your name! Their songs ring out with joy in the
trees and through the sky. They sing of Your glory, of Your beauty, of Your creativity.
And each song reflects the wonderful, wise, masterful craft of the Maker.

908

Here comes the sun, Lord! Radiant and warm, shining and pure—
its rays pierce the clouds and lift the fog off our country. I love
Your handiwork, and oh, how it brings me delight and joy!

909

I am struck by Your amazing grace—grace that is offered freely to everyone, everywhere. It's like nothing else. There is no one like You, Lord—so awesome in power and yet so willing to humble Yourself for us!

910

God, I am struggling with some doubts. I have lots of questions. I know You can hear me asking them—all the time they run through my head. Let me ask You today. . . .

911

Father, I don't feel like I quite fit in here. I long to live forever with You, in a world where I can understand that You are in total control. Here I so often feel on shaky ground. Help me to find someone to talk to, Lord.

912

You've painted tonight's sky, Lord, in brilliant, quiet shades of lavender and rose, coral and gold. What an artist You are! Help me to appreciate beauty wherever I find it, Lord. And let me praise You for it!

913

God, sometimes I don't feel like my abilities are as worthy or important as those of others. I just don't know what use I can be in Your kingdom. Yet I tell others all the time that everyone's gift matters. Help me to listen to my own advice, Lord.

914

Oh Lord! What a day! I can't even begin to count the mistakes I made. I'm so glad there will be another chance tomorrow! Thanks for giving me second and third and fourth chances, Lord.

915

The heavens declare Your glory, Lord. Such harmony in the songbird's voice, such brilliance in the golden rays of the sunlight, and such beauty painted in the patterns of the forest. You are a most glorious Creator, and I worship You!

916

God, I've been granted a position of authority, and honestly, I'm scared. God, help my fear to be healthy. Help it to keep me honest and humble and respectful. But also make me brave and wise enough to lead well.

917

God, my clumsiness has spread to my tongue. I've spilled some secrets and made a general mess of several of my relationships. Lord, help me repair what I've broken. Help me ask forgiveness. Help them to see my true heart.

918

Lord, as I help to tend to _____'s needs, I pray You stay by my side. Help me to recognize any pain before the cries reach my ears. Help me to see any change that indicates trouble. Guide my hands as I care for this precious soul.

919

Lord, we don't take time to listen to each other anymore down here. Please slow us down. Make us see one another. Dare us to care. Challenge us to cherish. Lead us to love.

....

....

....

....

....

....

....

....

920
Where are You, Lord? I can't hear You as well as I used to. I've wandered away into a wilderness of muddled thinking, listening to the voices of people who only want to make a profit. Clear my mind, Lord.

921
God, let me not be so worried about making people happy that I forget to please You. I give You these plans today, Lord. Tell me what You think of them.

922
Lord, it seems to be in style these days to say whatever comes to one's mind. But that is so often not helpful and not even true. God, help Your followers to be focused on speaking the truth. Help our words to be different from those of the world.

923
Jesus, what a friend You are! I can trust You completely. You are always here for me, every time I need You. You accept me with grace instead of crushing me with judgment. Help me to be a friend like You.

924
God, I'm waiting to hear back from some tests. I feel anxious and afraid. What is going to happen to me? Help me to know that, whatever comes, I am held by You.

925

My stomach is churning with fearful anticipation, Lord. This is a big day. A big moment. Can You reach down and quiet my twisting tummy? Can You smooth out my nerves? Can You still my grinding teeth? Come quickly, Lord, please!

926

This morning I will drench myself in Your Word and come out smiling. Let me spread the joy You plant in my heart, Lord. Give me words of praise, wisdom, and encouragement!

927

Remind me, Lord, not to just think before I speak but to pray. Let me turn over every sentence to Your Spirit. Instruct me in the words that will bring about Your purposes.

928

God, I want to read Your Word every day. I need it as much as food (or more). But somehow the minutes get away from me, and the hours disappear. And before I know it, the day is gone. Help me to make time with You a daily requirement.

929

Father, my house is creaking and the wind is howling. Storms are moving in quickly. I'm here all alone, and I'm frightened, Lord. Please calm my trembling hands. Comfort my heart. Give me courage and confidence, knowing You are with me.

930

Bitterness is so sickening, Lord. It poisons everything—my thoughts, my attempts at loving others, my willingness to do Your will. God, take the poison out of my life. Help me to be rid of it, once and for all. Let me start fresh, clothed in Your grace.

931

I'm working hard to meet my goal, Lord. I want to do my best. Help me not to panic as time gets short. Help me not to procrastinate in my stress. I need to focus on You. Lead me, Shepherd.

932

Lord, You walked into so many places where people hated You. You walked in with confidence and left a wake of grace. Help me to be brave like You, Lord. Help me to love strangers. Help me to speak to those who are prejudiced against me.

933

Psalm 27:3 says, "Though an army besiege me, my heart will not fear; though war break out against me, even then I will be confident." Plant Your words in my heart, Lord, so that when dread falls on me, I can conquer my fear!

934

I feel as alone as David facing Goliath. But all I need is You, Lord. You are my Savior, my deliverer, my Rock, my refuge. Thank You for never leaving me.

935

I know some people are watching how I live my life, Lord, and they think I'm crazy.
They think I'm naive for following You. I want to surprise them with Your power,
Lord. I want to bowl them over with the simple strength of Your grace.

936

My power lies in the faith-based boldness that only comes from knowing You
intimately. Lord, I keep going to bring glory to You. Let me boast in Your
greatness alone. I praise Your name, my strength and my deliverer.

937

God, I feel like my knowledge of the Bible is not adequate to convince anyone of
what I believe. I'm not even sure how to explain the gospel. Show me how to
learn more, Lord. Lead me to resources that will be trustworthy and true.

938

With all the amazing devices we have to help us navigate the world, Lord,
we still get lost so many times. But You've given us a map to guide our
steps in Your Word. Help me to depend on Your directions.

939

Help me to be like Nehemiah, Lord. He saw what needed to be done, and he
immediately acted. He stepped out in faith and gathered good helpers. He kept
going, even when so many tried to oppose him. That's what I want to do too.

940

God, why do I ever doubt Your power? You made the heavens and the earth, Lord. How is it I think You can't possibly shape me? I'm facing my own foolishness today, Lord. Forgive me for not walking out more boldly in faith.

941

Here I am again, Lord, kneeling at Your throne. Give me the grace, strength, energy, talent, compassion, peace, joy, intelligence, and faith that I need to meet the coming challenge. Thank You, merciful King.

942

God, I spend too much time thinking about how I look on the outside—how I look in others' eyes. Help me to remember that You don't look at the things people care about. You look at my heart. Please do what's needed to make that pleasing to You.

943

God, I am staggering under the weight of Your glory. Help me be worthy of speaking Your message. I give my words to You, Lord.

944

Lord, Your way is just and right. Help me to follow You with all my heart. Help me to keep my heart true so I will always do what pleases You. Help me to obey Your commands. I am devoted to Your Word.

945

God, bring to my mind this night all my sins. Show me my poor choices.
Display the error of my ways. Show me these things so that I can face them
and be forgiven. I want my thoughts to be pleasing to You, Father.

946

God, help me to remember today that everyone has a story. No one gets to
be the person they are in adulthood without having gone through some
struggles. And some are struggling even now—right in this minute.
Help me to remember that and be patient.

947

Teacher, I don't want to just read Your Word. I want to become passionate
about it! Set my spirit on fire, Lord. Turn my heart toward Your desires for
my life. Turn my eyes away from worthless things and keep my focus on You.

948

Scripture promises that I can have the mind of Christ so I can know and understand
Your words. God, direct my heart and mind as I study and pray. Show me the things
I need to comprehend. Make Your wisdom known to me. Thank You, Lord!

949

God, there are some stories and concepts in Your Word that are confusing to me.
There's so much I don't know about the world in which the Bible came to
be. Point me toward people who can help me understand more clearly.

....

....

....

....

....

....

....

....

950

God, I try so hard to stand on Your promises, but more often than not I find myself falling on my face. Help me not to lose sight of the plan You have for me. And when I fall, help me to get back up again and keep following You.

951

Lord, in every hello today, in every glance, in every handshake, let me impart a little bit of Your love. Bring peace to my heart so I can talk to people without fear and yet without being overbearing. Let me bring cheer wherever I go!

952

God, sometimes when I hear people talk about their happy childhoods, I feel envious. I wish I had that too. Let my scars from my past be a reminder of Your grace, Lord. I reaffirm my vow to make a difference in my world—to touch others with Your love.

953

God, I feel a little like Martha—always doing, never stopping. Always feeling like every duty has my name on it. Always resenting those who do not help. God, I want to be more like Mary today—more like Your disciples who just followed You and listened.

954

God, I went walking in Your rain today and was refreshed by the soft, cool drops of water. Each tiny drop does its part to cleanse this big, messed-up earth. Help me to be a small drop of blessing in someone's messy day today.

955

Lord, I panicked. I'm sorry. I just got overloaded with all the sensations
and I completely lost control. I want to handle things better next
time, Lord. Help me. Lead me to Your heart of peace.

956

I always think I have to come to You with something, Lord—some offering,
some praise, some thought, some worship. But today I just come empty-handed.
I come ready to be filled with whatever You have to give me.

957

I watched an eagle fly—soaring so easily through the sky. I want to be
like that eagle—riding on the wind, being moved by a power not its own.
I want to be moved by Your power, Lord, and lifted up to soar!

958

Almighty God, may the work of my hands honor You. May my feet take
me closer to You. May the strength in my body be used to build Your
kingdom. May the force of my will help me stand up for You.

959

God, You know how I like to argue. I even try to argue with You sometimes!
But today, I want to acknowledge my ignorance. I want to let go of my
arrogance. I want to hear You and others more clearly. Please help me, Lord.

960

God, I love to see the power in Your rainstorms. I love to hear the loud crashes of thunder and see the bright flashes of lightning, piercing our nights. I praise You and thank You for Your grand and breathtaking creation!

961

Lord, it is so easy for me to see the faults in others. I can do it without even thinking about it. But Jesus, You know how often I overlook those same faults in myself. Open my eyes, Lord! I'm trying!

962

God, I am just angry. And I can feel awful thoughts and hurtful words coming up to the top of my mind. Steer my thoughts in the right direction, Lord. Let me get control. Remind me that everyone makes mistakes—especially me!

963

Father, I don't want to be selfish. Help me to keep looking around me. Help me to put others' interests before my own. Help me to take care of others' needs before I think of taking care of mine. Help me to love like You.

964

Jesus, I know we live in a broken world. And I know, no matter how hard we try, we're never going to be able to fix this mess. Only You can heal hearts. Only You can mend families. Only You can defeat evil plans. Only You.

965

Lord, my tears come so easily sometimes. I get hurt, and the sting makes me cry out.
Today I just want You to remind me to feel others' pain as easily as I feel my own.

966

God, I am having a hard time forgiving someone. I keep trying, but then
the old feelings of bitterness and pain come back again. I want to be
free of this burden, Lord. Help me to be able to forgive like You.

967

God, I need Your wisdom. I have a hard decision to make. It's difficult, because there
seems to be no way out that won't hurt someone. Help me to find the path that
You want me to go on—even if it's the most rocky one. Give me courage, Lord.

968

Lord, I have to bid some friends farewell today. Please send them on their
way knowing they are loved. Please help me not to be so sad about them
leaving but to be glad for the new chapter of life they are beginning.

969

Lord, I heard a heartbeat today, and I want to thank You for life. Beautiful
life! Help me not to take any beating heart for granted. Help me to be
thankful for every second we have here to live and love together.

970

Father God, protect Your children. Watch over their steps. Guard their hearts. Bring peace to their minds. Help them to control themselves. Make them alert. Give them courage. Let them rejoice in You, Lord.

971

God, I have lost something and I need to find it. It's so frustrating, Lord, when my brain doesn't work the way that I want it to. Thank You for listening to my small problems, Lord. Guide me now.

972

God, I am fascinated today by the idea that You care for every sparrow. That You clothe every flower. That You know the name of every tree and every plant. That You know the number of hairs on my head. The details of Your glory are wonderful.

973

God, I saw something today that horrified and sickened me. I know You have probably seen worse. And I can't understand why people do such evil things. Wipe this vision from my memory, Lord, but don't let me forget the urgency I feel now to spread Your love.

974

Jesus, You didn't want to die. You didn't have to do it. You could have taken a different path. But You gave up everything for me. You not only died; You suffered. You bore humiliation and burning pain. How can I ever thank You for Your sacrifice?

....

....

....

....

....

....

....

975

Lord, I am hungry for knowledge of You. Direct my mind to Your Word.
Help me understand what the Bible has to say to me. Guide me now.

976

Have mercy on me, oh Lord! Your unfailing love surrounds me. Your great
compassion amazes me. Blot out my sins, Lord! Wash away anything impure
in me! Your Word is righteousness. Your judgment is holy. Let me hear it now.

977

Lord, this may be the only quiet moment I have today. I know I
can talk to You whenever I want to, but I especially love these
times when I can really concentrate on You. So let's do this.

978

Lord, when I am woken up in the night, let me remember that You never
sleep. You never slumber. You always watch out for me. Thank You, Lord!

979

Be my Lord, in running errands and in play. In going to the doctor and
in paying bills. In my job and in my home. In going out and coming in.
In waking up and lying down. Be the Lord of my everything.

980

Lord, help me to see whom I am influencing today. And please, Lord,
help me to shape my life into something that brings glory to You!
I want to be a good example for _____.

981

I rejoice in the funny bits of life. For harmless pranks and silly jokes. For baby giggles and big-kid chuckles. For guffaws and snorts and rolling-on-the-floor, laugh-out-loud moments. Thank You for laughter, Lord. Thank You for joy!

982

For the ones on the buses and subways and trains, I pray. For the ones flying overhead and the ones traveling on the seas, I pray. For the ones in the cars on the road with me, I pray. Help us all to get safely where we are going today, Lord.

983

Lord, thank You for clean water and healthy food. Thank You that I have so many simple blessings every day. Help me not to forget them. And help me figure out how I can share those simple gifts with others.

984

Lord, help me hold on to these small glimpses of heaven, and let their glory fill me with gladness. Help me to always keep Your hope before me. Help me to lead others to hope in You.

985

I don't want to be like that person who looks in the mirror and then forgets what they look like. God, help me to commit Your Word to memory. And then don't let me forget it, Lord. I want to obey Your commands. Today I will. . . .

986

Lord, I am shaking my head. I just can't figure people out sometimes. But help me to have compassion, even when I think others are making terrible decisions! Help me to remember that You must shake Your head at me too.

987

Christ is risen! Hallelujah! Lord, let me sit in the wonder of that moment of realization today. Let me imagine what it must have been like for Your disciples to discover that You were not in that tomb. You had defeated death, just as You said!

988

Lord, fill me, move me, teach me, lead me, shape me. Guide me with Your Word. Let my conscience remind me of what is right and good. I put my life in Your hands.

989

God, I went to bed angry last night, but help me to start off this day in forgiveness. Help me to be the first to say I'm sorry. Even though it is hard to do, help me to overlook offenses. Let me remember that love covers a multitude of wrongs!

990

God, I'm so glad that You still are willing to listen to me, even after I've sinned against You! I have a hard time letting go of my hurt feelings. Thank You for loving me with a love that never ceases. Help me to learn from that.

991

God, I'm nervous about telling my story. I want to be a good witness for You, but I'm just worried what people will say. Help me to get over these fears, Lord. Help me to speak out boldly on Your behalf.

992

Lord God, You are everything to me! You made the sun and the moon. You made the stars. You made the day and the night. You are forever and everywhere, inside me and all around. You are my all, my purpose, my heart. I give everything back to You!

993

Lord, some things that seem harmless could end up poisoning my spirit. Help me to be wise and discerning about the authors I read and the books and movies I allow to take hold of my thoughts. Guard my mind with Your goodness.

994

Sweet Holy Spirit! Stay with me today, all through the hours. Fill me with Your love and kindness. Let Your goodness overflow onto everyone I interact with this day.

995

Father in heaven, Your name is holy. Let Your kingdom come. Let Your will be done. Let me depend on You for my needs. Forgive my sins. Lead me away from the harm of temptation and out of the grasp of evil. You deserve all glory and honor and praise.

996

God, sometimes I talk too much and don't listen enough to what others have to say. Help me not to be like that with You today!

....

....

....

....

....

....

....

997
Lord, I get caught up in doing good things so much at times.
I act like my works are going to save me. But I know I am saved
only by Your grace. Help me to live like I know that.

998
Lord, may I love You with all my heart, mind, soul, and strength. Help
me to work out what that means in the day-to-day details of living and
working with others. Help me to love others more than I love myself.

999
Lord, bless this time of prayer. May it be my strength to face this day.
May it be a life-giving force that keeps me moving toward what
You desire for me. May it be the peace that calms my soul.

1,000
God, when I forget Your power, shock me. When I forget Your grace, restore me.
When I forget Your provision, refresh me. Holy Spirit, bring me back to the
awareness of the glory of You that I had when I first gave You my heart.

1,001
Lord, let the one who is thirsty come to drink from You. Let those who are dirty
come to be cleaned by You. Let all who are weary come. Let all who are sick
come. Let all who are strong come. And let You come. Come, Lord Jesus!

My Prayers

My Prayers